# A Taste of My Life

Chitrita Banerji is a Bengali-American writer who examines the relationships between memory, history, culture, religion and food in her works. She is the author of several acclaimed books on Indian food and culture, including *Eating India: An Odyssey into the Food and Culture of the Land of Spices* and *Bengali Cooking: Seasons and Festivals*. Her other works include the novel *Mirror City* and a biography of Sri Chaitanya. She is a two-time winner of a Sophie Coe Award in Food History and a member of the board of the Culinary Historians of Boston. She lives in Cambridge, Massachusetts.

## Advance Praise for *A Taste of My Life*

'Chitrita Banerji is an absolute master of the difficult art of writing autobiographically about food; she has very few equals in this field'

**– Amitav Ghosh**

'A book of complex flavours: by turns sad and joyous,
It leaves you licking your fingers and hungry for more'

**– Arvind Krishna Mehrotra**

'Can anyone "taste" someone else's life? It is difficult enough to recollect aromas and flavours – ephemeral sensual delights – savoured by oneself. But, with the help of a gifted illusionist, one can indeed travel back in time and across geographies to share the dreams, sorrows and joys of someone else. This is what Chitrita Banerji has accomplished in her delightful anthology of "remembrances of things past"'

**– Pushpesh Pant**

## Praise for Chitrita Banerji

'[Banerji is] a wonderful food writer'

– ***Gastronomica***

'Chitrita Banerji is one of those rare writers who can tease the meaning out of ordinary foods without ever seeming trivial, pretentious or self-indulgent ... [She] peels back the husk of triviality to reveal the history, culture, and emotional ballast that can reside in even the most everyday dish'

– ***Gourmet's Choptalk***

'One of the most evocative of Indian food writers, blending an exact understanding of techniques with an abiding curiosity about the many human stories behind the art of food'

– ***India Today***

# A Taste of My Life

## A Memoir in Essays and Recipes

Chitrita Banerji

PICADOR INDIA

First published in India in 2021 by Picador India
an imprint of Pan Macmillan Publishing India Private Limited
707 Kailash Building
26 K. G. Marg, New Delhi 110 001
www.panmacmillan.co.in

Pan Macmillan, The Smithson, 6 Briset St, Farringdon, London EC1M 5NR
Associated companies throughout the world
www.panmacmillan.com

ISBN 978-93-89109-85-6



Illustrations by Ranojoy Hazra



3 5 7 9 8 6 4 2



Typeset in Minion Pro by R. Ajith Kumar, New Delhi
Printed and bound in India by Replika Press Pvt. Ltd.

# Contents

# Author's Note

WHEN I FIRST CONSIDERED INCLUDING THESE PIECES IN one collection, I was not sure they could be arranged to reflect a thematic unity beyond the obvious one of food. They were written at different times and did not describe events in a linear, chronological format. On reflection, however, I realized that while food was a recurring theme, the pieces also reflected the universal experiences of curiosity, discovery, love, adventure, disappointment, heartbreak and loss. These experiences have provided the serendipitous arc of continuity that holds the essays in this collection together. The stories range from childhood to youth, through various stages of adulthood, adding up to the representation of a life.

Readers frequently expect actual recipes of dishes described in food-related pieces. In this collection, I chose to add recipes to all but the two concluding chapters.

I hope my readers will concur with this decision. Food is the stuff of life, the energy that propels us to action, movement and progress. Its absence signals the extinction of the flame, the inevitable conclusion of a journey.

# SUNDRIES

# Petal Vessel

ONCE, DURING A VISIT TO CALCUTTA, I WAS INVITED TO lunch by a woman whose reputation as a Bengali cook made me accept with delighted anticipation. The meal she served surpassed my expectations. What stood out above all the expensive fish and meat was her mochar ghanto, a fragrant dish consisting of banana blossom, or mocha, combined with tiny cubed potatoes, tinier coconut chips, chickpeas and spices. It's a classic of Bengali cuisine, which is known for its flavourful yet delicate use of spices and a wide range of ingredients.

My fellow guests avidly consumed every item on the table, but I noticed a teenage girl, who screwed up her face with acute dislike when she tasted the banana blossom. After lunch, the girl told me she'd never had it before and found the texture off-putting, though she didn't mind eating cucumbers, tomatoes, green peas and cauliflowers. What she loved most, however, was going out with friends and ordering french fries at a fast-food restaurant. Any budding notion I may have had about extolling the banana blossom to the younger generation instantly vanished.

Bananas have been around in India for aeons, and both the blossom and the pith inside the trunk were long ago integrated into the cuisine. A sixteenth-century biography of the Bengali mystic Chaitanya lovingly describes a banana blossom dish prepared for him in the house of a disciple. The fruit is not only universal nourishment but a prime offering for the gods. In Bengal, the plant has a mystique enriched by folklore. As a child, I loved the story of the beautiful Behula who sailed downriver in a banana raft all the way to the underworld to rescue her husband from the deadly vengeance of Manasa, the snake goddess.

Growing up, cooking lessons did not interest me, but watching my mother painstakingly prepare mocha was a delight that never waned. She took the large cone-shaped object and removed the reddish-purple leafy bracts. Under each nestled a cluster of tiny bananas which she put aside. Once all the purple layers had been stripped away, a smooth ivory-coloured centre was revealed. Along with the pile of baby bananas, this was chopped into small pieces and briefly boiled with salt and tamarind to leach away any bitterness.

For her much-anticipated mochar ghanto, she then heated mustard oil, tossed in bay leaves, whole cumin seeds and a few slit green chillies. As the fragrance of the spices filled the air, the banana blossom was added to the pot along with sautéed potatoes, coconut chips, and chickpeas, and seasoned with ground turmeric, ginger, cumin, coriander, chilli powder, salt and sugar. A final emulsifying touch of ghee and garom mashla was blended in just before the pot came off the fire. Bengali gastronomes consider this dish not only an eclectic pleasure but also a true test of a cook because of its mélange of textures – dense, chewy, soft and brittle – and the harmonious melding of spices. Every time I ate my mother's mochar ghanto, I agreed.

Sometimes, I saved a couple of the discarded purple bracts and pinned them together with toothpicks. Under my fingers they were amazingly seductive, soft as silk, smooth as velvet. The conical shape, slightly wider at one end, resembled a boat. In the evening, I'd go up to the roof, fill a large pail with water, place a small clay oil lamp left over from a Diwali festival on the purple leaf, and set it afloat. Usually, there was enough breeze to create little eddies on which the banana boat tossed around gently. I sat mesmerized, watching, wondering if it would capsize, but it never did, though the lamp went out after a while.

# Mochar Ghanto

## Ingredients

- 500 grams freshly chopped mocha (banana blossom), cooked and drained
- 60 grams chhola (Bengal gram), soaked overnight
- 170 grams ground coconut
- 2 medium potatoes, peeled and cubed
- 1 teaspoon whole cumin seeds
- 2 bay leaves
- 1 teaspoon each of turmeric and red chilli powder
- 1 teaspoon ground garom mashla (cinnamon, cardamom and clove)
- 3–4 green chillies, slit down the middle
- 4 tablespoons mustard oil
- 1 teaspoon ghee
- salt and sugar to taste

## Process

Mix the turmeric and chilli powder with the cooked mocha and set aside. Heat the oil in a pan and sauté the potatoes until light brown and set aside. In the same oil, throw in the bay leaves and cumin seeds, fry for a minute and throw in the soaked Bengal gram. After stirring for two or three minutes, add the cooked, seasoned mocha and stir for 3 or 4 minutes. Add the potatoes and half a cup of water and keep covered over medium heat until the water has almost evaporated. Now add the ground coconut, a teaspoon of salt and 3 teaspoons of sugar. The sweetness has to be a bit pronounced in this preparation. Stir thoroughly, add the ghee and the ground garom mashla, and taste (adjusting as needed) for the final salt and sugar balance before removing from the stove.

# Pleasure in a Cone

DURING MY HIGH SCHOOL YEARS, MY MOTHER WOULD sometimes ask me to accompany her to the market for evening shopping. The suggestion never failed to annoy me. I had no interest in the fruits, vegetables or spices that she planned to buy (fish and meat were morning purchases and usually bought by my father) and I also knew that the walk to and from the market would be peppered with questions about school work. My mother, a high school English teacher, was both strict and ambitious regarding my education. She also had an incredibly tenacious memory. Sanskrit grammar, which she had studied for her own school-leaving exams, could still be recalled with absolute clarity. For me, being quizzed on conjugations, declensions and other grammatical brain-teasers was absolute torture. Worse was when she interrogated me on the problems of inductive and deductive reasoning and the syllogistic mnemonics that were part of our logic curriculum. Inevitably, I was found wanting and had to endure pithy lectures on the dreary future that awaited me. In response, I sulked, hunched my shoulders, kept my eyes on the ground and trudged along, fuming with resentment at the unfair balance of power between adults and teens.

My mood lifted only when we made our way to the area of the market where the paan sellers were located. They did not sell ready-to-consume paan leaves that were twisted into the characteristic cone and filled with different ingredients, as specified by the customer. Those were sold by vendors in sidewalk stalls. Here, in the market, the unvarnished leaf was bought for domestic consumption. You took your supply home to make up in whichever way you fancied.

Every time we stopped at the paan shop my mother favoured, I marvelled at its visual effect. In the centre, on a flat wooden platform sat the seller, a middle-aged man in a white T-shirt and a chequered lungi pulled up to his knees. The mini-globe of his protuberant belly always made me think of the god Ganesha, but his all too human face was noticeable because of a red-stained mouth that never stopped chewing. This was a paan seller who loved his product. Around him on tiered shelves were baskets of heart-shaped leaves stacked one over the other, each with a long, extended stem jutting out. Unlike vendors of different vegetables, the paan seller was ensconced in a monochrome universe. Yet, the absence of multiple colours only emphasized the beauty of his product. Green is a default colour in a tropical landscape and its shades are beyond enumeration. While the vibrant emerald of a rice field or the dense, dark, brooding foliage of ficus, mango and lychee trees can strike the eye with potent immediacy, the discreet green tint of paan leaves laid out in layers has a subtle hypnotic effect.

To me it was a wonder that the paan seller could arrange his leaves with such exquisite, unvarying symmetry. The process starts early, the man told me, when I once asked him. As a commodity, paan is fragile, more so than greens and vegetables used in cooking. Damage from rough handling reduces its value. So the growers are extremely mindful about keeping their product undamaged. The leaves grow on vines that climb up on wooden frames, and are protected from extreme heat and sunlight with covers made of jute, dried grass or coconut leaves which are kept damp by regular spraying. Deriving from the Arabic term for cover or roof, these paan covers are called baraj in Bengali. When the leaves are ready, they are torn off one by one and placed inside woven baskets for transportation to the market. One time my mother and I happened to be there when two paan suppliers turned up at the vendor's stall. They unloaded their round covered baskets and our paan seller, still perched immovable on his stool, leaned forward to examine the leaves. Satisfied with the quality, he silently jerked his head to one side where a young man sat on a stool. It was his duty to deal with the business of money and, after a low-voiced discussion, he handed over the cash to the men. Our man, meanwhile, was busy counting out the twenty leaves of mithey paan – a variety only available in Bengal and the only one consumed by our family – that my mother had asked for. As on previous occasions, I was mesmerized by the hand-eye coordination that enabled him to pick out the twenty leaves and hold them out for my mother to inspect, all the while keeping them spread in a fan-like shape. She never asked him to change any of the leaves and, as soon as we got home, she would tend to them – washing each leaf carefully, placing all of them in a rimmed brass plate and covering them with a damp cloth. These were the days before we had a refrigerator and the cloth needed changing several times until all the paan was used up.

If food was the king for our large extended family of opinionated connoisseurs, paan was definitely the queen. My earliest memories include watching my mother and her sisters sitting in the large room on the second floor and preparing paan for family and guests on special occasions. Just like the paan seller's flair for arranging and holding the leaves, this too was a display of virtuosity bordering on art. The process was always the same. Take a leaf, fold it in the middle and pull the stem out so that the leaf bifurcates, then place one half on top of the other. This is followed by the addition of ingredients, starting with chun and khoyer – slaked lime and catechu paste – dabbed on the top half of the leaf with a slim brass pestle. Next were the chopped shupuri or areca nuts. The subtle rivalry between the sisters became evident when they peeked at each other's supplies of shupuri to determine whose was chopped the finest. Using the hand-held janti or shupuri chopper and reducing the hard, round, recalcitrant areca nut into the finest slivers was a feat of skill, strength and patience. Leisure hours were often spent chopping shupuri to stock up for many paan-making sessions. It took me a few years to figure out that my mother, the only working woman in the family, had the least amount of free time and her shupuris were never as fine as those of her sisters.

Last to be added was the jarda or scented tobacco, an item of infinite seductiveness for me because even touching it was absolutely forbidden. Hanging around the group preparing paan, I loved the moment when the tobacco containers were opened and a variety of aromas (based on each person's choice of brand) filled the air. I inhaled as much as possible, hoping to find the magical satisfaction the adults derived from those tiny, shredded leaves often coated in silver foil, but of course I never did. I could only listen to the arguments about the superiority of this or that brand, or, once in a while, observe the excitement surrounding the introduction of a new brand – particularly one from the distant, exotic realms of Lucknow and Benaras. There were times when my mother abandoned brand loyalty to go to one of the shops near our home where tobacconists made up jarda according to a customer's specifications. She would engage with the shopkeeper in a detailed discussion about the combination of tobacco and flavour that she wanted. Their words meant nothing to me, but I loved watching the man go into action, measuring out the shredded tobacco in a shiny aluminium container, weighing it on his miniature scales, transferring the tobacco to a large bowl and adding, drip by slow drip, mysterious attars and concoctions from small bottles. Afterwards, he proceeded to stir the mixture vigorously with his fingers. On and on he went until I wondered if the scent would leave the tobacco and stay on his hand. But that never happened. Whenever my mother opened that aluminium container – lid embossed with the name of the shop – I could smell the rich, multilayered perfume instilled into the tobacco.

The final step of paan-making was when my mother and aunts rolled up the leaf into a cone and this impressed me because of the swift expertise with which it was done. Sometimes I would ask for a leaf and experiment with it, but my attempts only resulted in a crunched-up mess of green. The mastery of paan was a mystery from start to finish.

Occasionally, a few paan leaves were prepared for guests or relatives who abjured tobacco. These innocent variations, containing fennel seeds, tiny sugar crystals, and silver-clad seeds of the black cardamom were judged to be suitable for all, including a child. On rare occasions, my pleading would result in me being given one. I chewed it with infinite pleasure, the sweet–sharp taste, the fragrance and the mélange of textures uniting blissfully in my mouth.

Strangely, neither of my grandparents ever had paan. At some point I discovered that the addictive leaf had been introduced in the family by my grandfather's guru, a devout Vaishnav, who came to visit us several times a year. Having to provide an endless supply of paan for him – the one indulgence this austere man allowed himself – resulted in my grandfather's children falling into the habit themselves. Once they had started, it was impossible to stop. My father, however, was a renegade. He was as devoted as any other person in the family to the guru (whom I called Barobaba), but he deplored the paan-chewing habit and there were many tart exchanges on this subject between him and my mother in the privacy of our rooms on the third floor. He never succeeded in weaning her off the habit.

Even having to go to work could not be a sufficient deterrent. Every morning she made up four or five of the paan cones and put them in a small oblong silver box, shaped like a book – an appropriate possession for a school teacher. It fit into her purse and during her off hours or at lunchtime, she could enjoy the refreshing pleasure of paan made for her particular palate.

It was when one of my younger aunts got married that I saw the paan leaf in a different light. It was a day of expectation and excitement, the house abuzz with sound and activity, family members, friends, servants rushing around, taking care of a multitude of tasks. The hired cooks had set up their equipment on the fourth-floor roof and the intense aroma of the items they were preparing drifted down to all the floors below from afternoon onwards. Although filled with a sense of anticipation, I was also aware of a strange nervousness.

This was a favourite aunt, almost a playmate, who had infinite patience for me. What would it mean when she got married? Although still a child, I knew that brides went away to live in their husbands' homes. But it did not seem real that life would continue in our house without my aunt being there. The afternoon wore on, evening came around. My aunt was locked into one of the rooms with a bevy of women who were helping her with dress, make-up, jewellery. I was not allowed anywhere near them. Finally, the bridegroom arrived with his relatives and friends and was brought upstairs to the room on the second floor where my mother and aunts used to sit for their mammoth paan-making sessions. The priest was there, the ritual objects and offerings were ready. It was time for the bride to be brought out for the ceremony. Hovering unobserved in a corner I saw some of my uncles and male cousins going into the room where my aunt was. After a while they came out. To my astonishment, she sat on a small wooden platform which was being carried by the men. I looked at her and couldn't find the person I knew and loved so much. Not only did the red-and-gold sari, gold-bordered red veil, heavy gold jewellery and a tiara made with white flowers and silver tinsel create a most unfamiliar image, it was also an image that repelled recognition. Two paan leaves, held up by my aunt, completely obscured her face. For one terrible moment, in spite of all the celebratory noise of blowing conch shells and feminine ululation, I thought she had disappeared forever and the figure that was being brought in for the wedding was someone I didn't know. Eventually, I was relieved to see the dear familiar face again when they took the paan leaves from her and she was seated in front of the groom, waiting for her father to ceremonially give her away. But some part of the anxiety caused by her appearance lingered for a long time. Off and on, when I watched my mother and other family members preparing paan and chewing it with enjoyment, I would wonder why those beautiful leaves had seemed like a barrier, shutting me out of a phase of my childhood during which my aunt and I had danced together, played hide-and-seek, shared sweets and sung silly little songs. Her youthfulness was left behind with the paan leaves as she made ready for life in another house and I was left with the first sense of the permanence of loss that life sends us so often.

Decades have gone and taken my mother and many of my relatives with them. I still have that little book-shaped silver paan box my mother carried in her purse when she went to work. Once in a while I open it and look inside. Is it my imagination, or is it true that a faint aroma of the Bengali mithey paan combined with my mother's personal blend of perfumed tobacco still lingers? I close my eyes and inhale, stepping into a leafy green realm where the perennial mysteries of scent, flavour, colour, addiction and the unseen beauty of a bridal face rise up around me.

# Addiction-free Mithey Paan

## Process

For each person, take one fresh, undamaged paan leaf. Fold it and gently pull the stem down until the leaf separates into two pieces. Place one half on top of the other, with the deeper green side facing upward. Gently coat the central part of the top leaf with slaked lime and catechu paste. Sprinkle a pinch of finely chopped betel nut on the paste. Then add (according to your preference) small portions of fresh-ground coconut, a pinch of fennel seeds, a pinch of sugar crystals, a few seeds of black cardamom and, if available, pieces of sweet, soft, fermented betel nut covered with edible foil.

Gently fold the two halves together to form a cone, tucking in the ends at the top, and fasten with a couple of whole cloves.

# Small, Round Things

LIVING IN THE WEST, I HAVE GROWN ACCUSTOMED to thinking of summer as berry season. The indolent pleasures of repeatedly dipping into bowls of sun-warmed blueberries, strawberries, raspberries or gooseberries and absorbing their sweet juiciness affirms, as nothing else, that the North American winter has been left behind. Once upon a time, though, I had a life where it was winter that was the harbinger of a season of small, delicate, flavourful fruits, which could be consumed as endlessly as the berries of summer. In tropical Bengal, January came with the delicious promise that mutated and extended into the next eight months.

The first of these small fruits, topa kul and narkel kul, came with a bind. Bengali Hindus are forbidden to eat them until Saraswati Puja, when the goddess of learning and music is worshipped with great fanfare. The date varies from year to year, determined according to the Bengali calendar and the phases of the moon. In the years when the fifth day of the waxing winter moon in the month of Magh happened to fall in February instead of January, children and adults in my observant Hindu family were sorely tested. The memory of the previous year's pleasures filled us with the itch to bite into these sweet-and-sour fruits displayed in the Calcutta markets and sidewalk stalls. Available, yet untouchable, they were a daily invitation to transgression.

The sight of sceptics, unbelievers and non-Bengalis insouciantly purchasing the fruits – worse, popping a few into their mouths as they walked off – became the proverbial snake in the garden, underscoring both the temptation and the pain of deprivation for me and my cousins. Why couldn't we do the same, we wondered; why did we have to follow these silly rules? But a greater fear held us in thrall. If we lost Saraswati's favour by eating kul ahead of her arrival, we would be doomed to a lifetime of ignorance and illiteracy. Silly or not, it was a belief that had been thoroughly inculcated in us. Even in the years when the fruit came early and the goddess was unusually tardy, all we could do was watch sorrowfully as the mounds of rotting fruit piled up outside the markets, waiting to be taken away by the municipal garbage trucks.

Most years, though, the pleasure was timely, honed to perfection by a short period of desiring what we could not have. The goddess sailed in serenely at the peak of the kul season, borne by her carrier, the white swan. Dressed in white and gold, she held a book in one hand and a veena in the other. While the priests or family elders worshipped the image with all the appropriate rituals, we children – made to fast until the puja was over – focused avidly on the large plates of fruits and sweets set out before the goddess. Soon enough, it was time for mortals to taste these offerings that Saraswati had supposedly graced with her acceptance.

We always ate the pale-green oval narkel kul first. Its firm white flesh and sweet–sour taste toyed delicately with the tongue, leading us down the path of overindulgence. Its cousin, the topa kul, was more challenging to the palate. Smaller and rounder, its red-skinned form contained flesh that was usually too tart for comfort. It was therefore just the right fruit to be made into pickles and chutneys in combination with spices and oil or date palm sugar. But the simplest way to make topa kul into a treat that made the tongue shiver with pleasure was to pop them open (one squeeze was enough), toss them liberally with salt and leave them on balcony or window sill or roof for a few days to dry in the sun. The treatment transformed the slipperiness of the inner pulp into an elastic consistency without impairing the fragrance, while the parched skin yielded its layered flavour and texture only after prolonged chewing. During holidays and weekends, my cousins and I could think of few better ways to spend a lazy winter afternoon than by sitting on the balcony or roof, our backs toasted by the balmy tropical sun, making our way through a pile of salted topa kul.

The warming southwestern breezes that usher in the briefest of springs to Bengal blow away the two kinds of kul to make room for a couple of fruits that are exquisitely delicate in both taste and appearance. Unlike most berries, the jamrul is neither round nor oval. Instead, it is shaped like a small bell, narrow at the stem and flaring out into a wide mouth where the flesh is folded into four petal-like formations. It is more of a pleasure to hold and look at a jamrul than to eat it. The colour is white, washed with an undertone of pale green, and the flesh carries the translucency of expensive jade. The taste matches the coolness of the look. Biting into a jamrul is like having a mouthful of warm granita, if you can imagine that. As you eat, the flesh breaks up into crunchy yet moist crystals, releasing a juice that is almost like water. But then the elusive flavour – like the night-blooming flowers of the hasnahana vine, like the essence of green tea – emerges, tantalizes for a brief moment, then disappears. It makes the jamrul an ideal fruit of intermission, helping Bengalis segue from the delicious coolness of winter into the scorching heat of summer.

But it was the golapjam (no relative of the gulab jamun served in Indian restaurants abroad) that became my favourite fruit at this time of year as I grew out of childhood into my teens. The reason could be its comparative rarity and very brief availability. For observant Hindus in Bengal, the calendar is dotted with numerous occasions that require one to fast – for a day or part of a day – with or without drinking water. When daughters reach puberty, mothers and grandmothers start inducting them into the intricate rituals of the believer's life. Fasting, however difficult it might be for a young person, is often required. Like teenagers everywhere, I too precipitated many battles because of my propensity to question instructions, to flout the norms of 'good' behaviour. But instead of relenting, my elders only pressed me harder to conform.

Once, when I was told I would have to fast all day in honour of some obscure deity, I felt particularly put upon. It was, I remember, a holiday. There was no school to go to, no immediate prospect of escape from the house. Furious and seething with contempt for adults who were always preaching the value of a scientific education and yet enforcing superstitious practices, I flounced upstairs and banished myself to the roof. From its fourth-floor elevation, I glowered at the cityscape spread out before me and spun my dreams of escape and autonomy. But even in spring, even when you are consumed with righteous rage, the Bengali sun is hard to tolerate too long. After a couple of hours, I had to slink downstairs to seek solace in solitude with a favourite book.

Passing through the central lobby on the third floor, into which all the rooms opened, I came to a sudden halt. On a corner table sat a small shopping bag, the kind our servants took to the market. How it came to be there I could not fathom, since the kitchen and dining areas were on the second floor. But there it was, a bag bulging with objects, and I had to investigate. Inside were two bunches of red-leaf notey shak, packets of spices done up in newspaper and twine, a bunch of small bananas and a cluster of golapjams. Almost involuntarily, I picked up a fruit and brought it to my nose. The golapjam gets its name from its scent – the exquisite perfume of the rose. Like the jamrul, its colour is a pale, whitish green, but the edible skin is opaque and slightly rough. If you rattle it vigorously, you can feel the loose seed rattling about inside. Before I knew what had happened, half the fruit was in my mouth, filling it with a delicate sweetness that went beyond words. Half terrified and half delighted, I swallowed the mouthful before realizing how dangerous it was to stand there and be discovered feasting instead of fasting. Quickly I ran to my room, but not before I had stolen two more fruits from the bag. Behind locked doors, I could eat safely, and as I did, any fear I might have felt was replaced by a brazen satisfaction at having broken the rules without being discovered. The feeling was even sweeter than the juicy flesh of the golapjam, and though I did not know it then, it was the first deliberate expression of unorthodox impulses that plagued my family for years to come.

I can't say doubt never raised its head. A teenager does not have unfailing reserves of conviction. But I did have enough will to eventually squelch the doubt and the fear of retribution that arose in moments of weakness. Perhaps it was the power of the monsoon rains – not merely that year, but over successive years – that washed away the lingering second thoughts by affirming the rightness of enjoying and satisfying the senses. To my mind, there is no other season like the Bengali monsoon. When the dark army of clouds rushes in from every corner of the sky, they convey an awesome sense of power – power that quenches the seemingly unending pain of summer in a few short hours. Through the three and a half months that the monsoon usually rules over Bengal, the rain comes and goes, just as the heat and humidity also rear their ugly heads. But that first extraordinary sense of liberation lingers for many weeks.

Among the many delectable offerings of the season are two small, piquant fruits, the kalojam (known as jamun in other parts of India) and the karamcha. The unique taste of the kalojam, astringent yet sweet, lingers long after the fruit has been eaten. As for its deep purple colour, bordering on black, it has a durability unmatched in the fruit kingdom. A pleasurable session of devouring kalojam is advertised to the world afterwards by a purple-stained tongue. In colonial times, there were many stories of the horrified reaction of the British sahib confronted by his subordinates' darkly tinted lips and tongue. As a city girl, I ate only kalojam bought from the market. But watching the dark monsoon sky, I used to wonder whether it was indeed more pleasurable, as I had often read, to be outside the city, under a kalojam tree, eating the ripe fruit that had fallen on the ground.

The other fruit of the monsoon, the karamcha, begins to appear at the tail end of summer but becomes abundant with the rains. Each year, its beauty struck me anew. The colour, graduating delicately from white to blushing pink, is worthy of the pure oval of its form. Its tartness, though, demands a brave palate to consume it raw. Dipping it in salt makes it easier. Bengalis have found numerous ways of combining karamcha with fish and vegetables to produce classic dishes. The roe of Bengal's favourite fish, the hilsa, delicious on its own, is singularly enhanced by the addition of this mischievously tart fruit. But as in the winter, with the tart topa kul, the leisurely afternoons of the monsoon are ideal for savouring a salty, spicy pickle made with karamcha. It is a sure-fire remedy for the inertia and lack of appetite that can occasionally ail one in the later part of the rainy season. Metamorphosed by salt, oil and spices, it ironically evokes the dry heat of early summer and knocks you out of lassitude.

That may be why the folk imagination of Bengal has invested the karamcha with magical powers to halt the rain. In the bustling, urban landscape where I grew up, the idea was a charming absurdity. Even in my family where religious rituals and observances were so important, there was little to connect us with the kind of beliefs that were deeply rooted in the soil. I remember going with my father to see *Pather Panchali*, the first film in Satyajit Ray's Apu trilogy. In an unforgettable scene, little Apu and his teenage sister Durga are caught far from home in a violent monsoon downpour that looks like it will never end. They have no umbrella, no shelter. Worse, they know they will face the wrath of their mother for having strayed too far from home. Desperate, drenched, shivering and anxious about her little brother catching a chill, Durga repeatedly chants a nonsense rhyme that is supposed to put a stop to the deluge. It invokes a karamcha sitting on a lime leaf and commands the rain to go away. Durga's utter desperation is also the measure of her faith.

When we came out of the theatre, I laughed at the absurdity of it. My father, the gentlest of men, who hardly ever spoke harshly to me, gave me a look of anger and sadness. How could I know, he asked, what life was like in rural Bengal in the early part of the twentieth century, a time when a telegraph pole or a fast-moving train were miraculous sights? Even later, during his own boyhood, when he spent school vacations in the village, he was impressed by the immense sense of difference conferred by place. It did not take long, he said, to lose the confidence of urban life, the sense of autonomy and control that came from having electricity, running water, mechanized transportation, telephones. In the rural world, the unpredictable and the uncontrollable were always present on the edge of consciousness. Nonsense rhymes were as good as anything else to get you out of trouble.

It was a humbling moment for me. I tried to visualize a life in a time and place so very different from my own. I imagined myself to be Durga, alone and far from home under an open sky that poured sheets of water on me. I thought about getting lost, being sick. Yes, I would chant that rhyme too, with desperation, with faith. The karamcha and the lime leaf were both magical and real.

Some years, the monsoon is cruel to Bengal. Instead of happy rejuvenation, it brings numerous floods. Even the cities can be under protracted siege. Urban streets become streams. People in villages are marooned on roofs and treetops. Engorged rivers wash away homes and settlements. In those years I think of all the young Bengali girls who may have invoked the blushing pink karamcha and vivid green lime leaf to ward off the ruinous rain. I hold them close in my heart.

## Topa Kuler Ambol

### Ingredients

- 200 grams topa kul
- a pinch of whole mustard seeds
- one whole dried chilli
- sugar and salt to taste

### Process

Wash the topa kul well, removing the stems. Heat a tablespoon of mustard oil and throw in the chilli and the mustard seeds. As soon as the seeds sputter and emit their fragrance, add the topa kul and stir well for 2 to 3 minutes. Add a little bit of salt, one and a half cups of water, cover and cook for 10 minutes. Uncover and check if all the topa kul has softened and become edible. You can press with the spatula to see if the fruits split easily, revealing the seeds inside. This is also the time to decide if you want to add more water, depending on the consistency of the ambol that you want. Add a quarter cup of sugar, cover the pot and cook for 5 more minutes. Then taste to check whether you want to add more salt and sugar. An ambol should be much more tart than a chutney. Adding more sugar depends on the cook's palate. The natural viscosity of topa kul will create a sauce with body and the natural fragrance of the fruits will combine with that of the spices to create an intensely flavourful dish.

## Karamchar Chutney

### Ingredients

- 200 grams karamcha
- mustard oil
- 1½ teaspoon finely chopped ginger
- one dried red chilli
- 200 grams sugar
- salt to taste

### Process

Split each karamcha in half and remove the seed from inside. Once all the karamchas have been cut, wash thoroughly, rinsing in 2 or 3 changes of water. Heat some water in a pan. Once the water comes to a boil, add all the karamcha, bring to a boil again and remove from the stove. Drain the water. This process is necessary because these blushful beauties have an inherent astringency mingled with tartness that has to be got rid of. Heat a tablespoon of mustard oil in a pan, add the chilli and chopped ginger and fry for a couple of minutes before adding a little water and all the sugar. Once the sugar has melted into a thick syrup, add the karamcha. Stir in some salt, a pinch at a time, and keep tasting the mixture. Let the chutney come to a boil again, taste the sauce and the texture of the fruit, and remove from the stove. This chutney should have an intense sweet-and-sour taste and the fruits should be coated thickly in syrup.

# Double Roti

THE VERY FIRST SANDWICH SERVED TO ME IN THE United States petrified me with its size and heft. I had just arrived from Calcutta and was going to spend ten days in a Pennsylvania town with one of my uncles and his American wife, before travelling to Cambridge to start graduate school. This, my uncle had written to my anxious parents, would be the easiest way for me to segue into a new life.

The day after my arrival, he took me out to see 'America' at close quarters. After a long, pleasurable morning replete with historical sights and novel, sometimes eye-popping, encounters – the dazzling, escalator-laced interior of an American department store was a splendid antidote to the musty, neon-lit, static shops I was familiar with – my uncle decided it was time to eat. We went to one of his favourite restaurants, famous for its sandwiches.

The long list of options on the menu was enough to make my head whirl. Until then, my idea of a sandwich was two pieces of thin-sliced, crustless, buttered white bread – yes, bread in the Western sense was always as white as the Europeans who had introduced it to India, and if one wanted a whole wheat product, one could always eat a homemade chapati – that enclosed either vegetables like sliced cucumber and tomatoes, or boiled eggs that had been sliced or mashed or, the most opulent option (available usually in restaurants), sliced chicken. When sandwiches were made at home, my mother would sometimes strive for variety by frying an egg until the yolk had set solid and put it between the slices of bread. Or she made an omelette and used that as a filling, trimming off the untidy ends. Fillings of meat like ham or beef, regardless of expense, were unthinkable in observant Hindu homes like ours, and sliced cheese was not commonly available in the markets in those days.

The one unvarying assumption, however, was that the sandwich was either a light accompaniment with afternoon tea – as we had learned from the British – or a convenient snack, along with fruits and something sweet, to put in the lunch boxes we carried with us to school. In sixties' Calcutta, there was no such thing as school lunch. We ate our main meal of the day – the

Bengali lunch consisting of rice, dal, vegetables and fish or meat – at home, at the ungodly hour of eight-thirty or nine, before boarding the school bus. The contents of our modest-sized lunch boxes therefore provided sufficient sustenance for the rest of the day. Outside the school, the sandwich, a quintessentially British item, also carried an aura of Westernized elitism. Teatime guests in ordinary Bengali homes like mine were likely to be offered samosas, fritters and sweets, not sandwiches. There was no need for the sandwich to change its identity from snack to meal, as it had in the West, even though the term itself, like many other foreign words, had become incorporated into most Indian languages. In the early days of colonial rule, however, when Indian servants were first taught to prepare this peculiar item for their European masters, and long before Indian families added it to their menu, they referred to it as 'double roti'.

That first afternoon in America I sat in the restaurant with my uncle, scanning a long list of sandwiches, and found many terms I couldn't comprehend. Even bread wasn't simply bread. Yes, I knew about buns and rolls, but words like rye and pumpernickel totally fazed me. My uncle, a food enthusiast from his college days in Calcutta, sat grinning at my bewilderment. He was willing to explain but he wouldn't order for me. This, in his opinion, was one of the many moments in America where I had to be adventurous, jump into the unfamiliar and find my balance. Not being too fond of boiled eggs, I decided to order the chicken salad sandwich which seemed the least intimidating option after egg salad. When the waitress arrived with our plates, my uncle's pastrami on rye failed to elicit the expected questions from me. I was dumbstruck by the dimensions of the item sitting before me.

Everything about it contradicted the fundamental notion of the sandwich as something light and simple. Even the slices of bread, although familiarly white, were three times the size of any sliced bread I had eaten in India. The sandwich had been cut diagonally to make two triangles and each could have sufficed as a filling meal. I saw the greenery poking out from the sides and discovered that lettuce was a common addition to a sandwich. As for the filling bursting out from between the bread, it was literally worlds apart from the delicate slices of meat I had been expecting. The American chicken salad, with its chopped chicken, chopped celery and profusion of mayonnaise, challengingly flaunted its unfamiliarity. I was prepared to believe it was tasty, but the wet, mushy texture did not invite me to find out – until I gathered my courage and took a bite.

It was a memorable meal. As I had expected, half of

the sandwich, not to speak of the french fries on the side, was enough to contain my hunger. The lushness of the chicken salad, so different from the chaste pieces of chicken I had anticipated, lingered in my mouth like a strange, sinful pleasure while I realized, with some embarrassment, that the trick of holding and eating a giant American sandwich without making a mess was something I would have to learn by practice. But what I have discovered since then is that responding to the initial challenge – urged on by my uncle's quizzical smile – brought me a permanent source of gratification. Countless American sandwiches later, including the burgers, the BLTs and the ones filled with thick-piled slices of cured or roasted meats, it is the simple chicken salad sandwich that remains my favourite, provided the mayonnaise is applied with discretion.

That afternoon, my sandwich also brought home to me the reality of America as the proverbial land of milk and honey. Looking around at the customers, I saw that most of them were ordinary, middle-class folk, not swanky members of the elite. Yet, they could easily afford to pay for lavish portions of high-protein, high-calorie food. Some of their meals were far bigger than my plate of sandwich. Chicken, my uncle told me, was ubiquitous in the American diet, being a relatively cheap source of protein. I thought about the land I had left behind. For middle-class Indian families like mine, chicken was an expensive commodity, a treat reserved for special occasions or for feeding a convalescent. I remember one friend telling me that in her house the price of a chicken was never taken out of the regular food shopping budget. Her mother collected the money she got by selling old clothes and newspapers to the itinerant buyers who came by each month, until it added up to the price of a good-sized chicken – a treat, not simply a meal.

On the rare occasions when people like us did splurge and eat out at restaurants that served so-called 'Continental' (read Western) food, the chicken sandwich consisted of thinly sliced bread (each piece no more than three inches by three inches after the crust had been removed), sparingly buttered and enclosing several slices of plainly cooked skinless, boneless chicken. Although the Bengali meals we ate at home were seasoned with a whole gamut of spices, I relished the plainness of the chicken in this sandwich. I can still taste the one served at a restaurant near our house which had a reputation for high-quality Western food. The meat had an ineffable delicacy, a melting-in-the-mouth tenderness that dismissed all desire for spice. Some people liberally poured ketchup on their plates and dipped the sandwich before taking each mouthful, but to me that seemed heretical. The only seasoning I ever felt like adding was a few sprinkles of fresh-ground pepper.

Nostalgia being no match for immediacy, my continuing years in America diluted the memories of those unvarnished chicken sandwiches almost to the point of erasure until one of my visits to Calcutta. I had gone to see a film with a couple of old friends. When we emerged, it was exactly the hour when the day dips into the western darkness and yet it is still light. Parched and hungry, we stood on the sidewalk watching the rush-hour Calcutta traffic, sometimes whizzing by at suicidal speed, sometimes slowing down to a crawl. Office workers on foot crossed the street with absolute disregard for their safety or survival, assuming that a half-raised arm would bring the speeding cars to a stop. It didn't take long to decide that a retreat from this chaotic diesel- and gasoline-infused whirlwind was in order, preferably a retreat with refreshments. Tea and sandwiches – the same vision came to all three of us. Across the street loomed a McDonald's, the first one in Calcutta, but my friends, like me, had no desire to pass under those golden arches. Instead, we found a restaurant that promised both quietness and the traditional teatime snacks we wanted. Sitting in the dim, comfortably shabby interior, I tried to resurrect in my mind the exact taste and flavour of those delicate chicken sandwiches that I had once savoured. Was it at all realistic to expect anything similar after so many years? The first discordant note sounded when the waiter taking our order asked if we would like cheese to supplement the different fillings of our sandwiches. Cheese, I was told, meant the processed slices a la Kraft that a local Indian company called Amul marketed with great success. One of my friends opted for the cheese with her tomato sandwich, but I wanted nothing to modify the plain chicken filling between the slices of buttered bread. When the plates arrived, however, the first glimpse was almost as much of a jolt as the first American sandwich I had eaten with my uncle. The bread was still thin-sliced and white, but the pieces were significantly larger. I lifted one corner to peek at the chicken and found it slathered with mayonnaise. I took a bite with resignation instead of anticipation. Gone was the delicate buttery taste and even the texture of the chicken pieces had changed. Instead of the remembered emollient tenderness, I encountered dense, juiceless, fibrous shreds of meat.

It might have been wiser to accept right away that just as you can't go home again, nothing can really taste the way you remember it. But this disappointing meal simply filled me with a mulish determination to keep looking until I found a replica of the sandwich that had once provided such a delicate pleasure. In the years since, I have ordered chicken sandwiches numerous times during my visits to India – in small restaurants, multi-starred restaurants, cafes, hotel bars, even airport lounges. I have even revisited the restaurant where I went as a schoolgirl and fell in love with the taste and notion of a chicken sandwich. Each time, I have been let down for different reasons. In most eateries, especially in the American-style cafes mushrooming all over the urban areas, the sandwiches are enormous – closer to a meal than a snack – and the chicken, instead of being thin-sliced, is chopped and drowned in mayonnaise. In some places, the bread is porous and tasteless as paper. Elsewhere, I have encountered extraordinary combinations of spices added to the chicken and coexisting with the oily blandness of badly made mayonnaise – no doubt an attempt to create fusion food.

These days, I am mostly ready to believe that the Calcutta sandwich I remember is no more obtainable than a mirage. Still, I haven't given up the chase. On each visit to India, the chicken sandwich of my youth continues to tantalize me like the fabled golden deer that lures one into unfamiliar byways with the promise of gratification.

# Chicken Sandwich from Memoryland

## Ingredients

- 4 large pieces of white bread, as soft and pillowy in texture as possible
- white breast meat of young chicken, poached to a tender consistency
- butter, salted or unsalted, according to individual preference
- whole black pepper
- salt to taste

## Process

Remove the crusts from the bread slices. Cut each slice diagonally in half. Butter the slices lavishly. Cut the chicken into slices, as thin as possible. Season with salt and freshly ground black pepper. Place the chicken slices (as many as you wish) between two triangles of bread to form one sandwich. Repeat with all the remaining slices of bread and chicken. Serve with potato chips and hot tea.

# A Sweet Fragrance in Winter

THE ROW OF DATE PALMS STOOD LIKE SENTINELS NEXT to an empty field readied for the sowing of winter vegetables. Their tall trunks displayed scores of scars – evidence of years of tapping for sap – and the sharp, spiky fronds sprouting from their tops resembled the knotted hair on the heads of witches that inhabited the fairy tales of my childhood. On the other side of the trees lay an old family graveyard, unkempt with high grass, wildflowers and shrubs through which peeked grey and white headstones, an unusual element in a Bengali Muslim cemetery. How fitting, I thought, that these trees whose ornery appearance so belied the sweet redolence of their sap should stand between the mysteries of life and death.

I was visiting a friend's house in a Bangladesh village famed for the taste and aroma of the liquid syrup processed from the sap of the date palm tree as well as the solid fudge-like chunks made by boiling it down – both called khejur gur in Bengali. Having grown up in a big, bustling Indian city like Calcutta, I had never seen khejur gur being harvested and processed, although from my earliest days I had been aware of its near-mythic status in Bengali gastronomy. When I received the invitation to visit, I simply could not resist the opportunity to observe the transformation of the clear palm syrup into rich, brown liquid gur, and then into solid, bowl-shaped rounds of patali. As the December evening deepened, I turned to go inside my friend's ancestral home, filled with a pleasurable anticipation of the morning to come. My host had promised to wake me early with the syrup that would have accumulated at night in the clay pots suspended from the tree trunks. Nothing, according to the locals, was more refreshing than that pale, clear, unprocessed liquid. Not even orange juice, said my friend. However, it has to be drunk almost with the first light of dawn. The warmth of the sun, even the mild sun of a tropical winter, starts a process of fermentation which affects the purity of the taste.

In modern Bengali parlance, gur stands for any unrefined sugar, whether produced from sugarcane juice or the sap of the date or other types of palms. While sap from coconut, palmyra and sago palms is harvested from the spathes they produce during flowering season, it is the trunk of the khejur or date palm tree that has to be tapped for its sap.

The history of sugar production in India goes back to antiquity, as can be seen from references to sugarcane in Sanskrit texts written as early as 1500 BCE. The etymology of the terms for various kinds of sugar bears testimony to a long-time gastronomic presence. The term gur, deriving from the Sanskrit guda, meaning ball, was used to describe the round discs made from either coagulated cane juice or palm sap. The generic meaning of the word, however, was later contested by the great fifth-century physician Charaka, who declared that guda was derived from Gauda, as parts of Bengal were called in antiquity. Given the Bengali reputation both as sweet makers and passionate consumers, Charaka's theory seems plausible. The ancients also used the term khanda (from which the English word candy is derived) to designate large lumps of sugar. What is more, the English word sugar stems from the Sanskrit sharkara, which originally meant gravel or pebble, an apt description of a granulated sweetener. Indians probably discovered how to make granulated sugar from cane juice as early as fourth century BCE. Alexander the Great's soldiers described with amazement a product that resembled 'stones the colour of frankincense, sweeter than figs or honey', clearly a reference to brown sugar crystals.

The Bengali/Indian date palm, *Phoenix sylvestris* (kharjur in Sanskrit, hence khejur in Bengali) is related to the better-known palm tree of the Middle East, *Phoenix dactylifera*, which is thought to have originated in the desert oases of Africa and Southwest Asia. The trees of the Middle East are justly famous for their juicy, substantial dates. The Bengali date palm, unlike its desert-bred cousin, prefers moist, alluvial soil and a humid climate, and the dates it bears are of a comparatively poor quality. It is cherished and grown primarily for its sap. Unlike maple syrup in North America, which is mostly featured on the breakfast table, poured over waffles and pancakes and also used as a flavouring for ice cream or made into fudge candy, khejur gur has a starring role in Bengali desserts throughout the winter when the tapping and processing take place. Unlike sugarcane juice, date palm syrup cannot be made into sugar crystals because of its chemical structure.

When date palm syrup is harvested in the Middle East and the countries of Southeast Asia, it is not for use as a sweetener but to be fermented and made into liquor. Consequently, there is a marked difference in the management of these trees. The Bengali way of cutting and tapping the tree is more environmentally sustainable, with the cuts being made in the trunk instead of in the head. This mutilates the trees far less and allows them to regenerate regularly. In the rural economy of Bengal, well-kept trees are an asset that can be used to pay off debts or serve as part of a marriage dowry.

Tapping for gur in Bengal (both in the Indian state of West Bengal and in Bangladesh) begins in late October, after the aman rice (the year's major crop) has been safely harvested and farmers enjoy relative leisure as they prepare their fields for planting winter vegetables and the spring or boro rice crop. The tapping season lasts until late February, with the best quality sap being produced in December and January. Although gur made from the earliest tapping is not the best in terms of flavour and taste, it is valued as an ingredient (along with the newly harvested rice) for offerings made to gods during the harvest festival of Nabanno.

Tapping is considered an art, and every village has one or two masters who are famed for their touch. Expert tappers, sometimes called gachhis (from the Bengali word gachh, meaning tree), climb up the rough trunks, carrying one or more sharp scythe-like knives in baskets tied around their waists. Their first task is to peel off all the old leaves below the crown and trim the outer tissues covering the trunk. This is done several times over a period of a week to ten days, so that only a few layers of inner tissue are exposed at a time and then allowed to be grown over with a webby bark. Too deep an exposure of the tree's insides is fatal. Finally, when the tapper judges the time to be right, he carefully makes a V-shaped notch, inserts a slender piece of slit bamboo into the narrow point of the notch, and positions a clay pot underneath so that the sap can flow into it throughout the night. The pot is taken down in the morning, but sometimes farmers are thwarted by mischievous and daring children who get there at daybreak, pull down the pot, drink the juice and replace the empty container before scampering off.

My day in the village began as expected – with a tall glass of fragrant, clear palm sap. Its uncloying sweetness was astonishing. By late morning, it was time for the gur makers to start their work. The sap was poured into a large iron wok which was placed on top of a wood-fired furnace. As it kept boiling, the surface was covered with froth which the gur maker repeatedly skimmed off with a ladle, just the way one does when cooking lentils. In about a quarter of an hour, the liquid began to thicken, the colour changed to a rich, dark brown, and the characteristic aroma of khejur gur filled the air.

Processed gur comes in three categories. The treacly liquid resulting from the initial boiling is called nolen (derived from the Turkish word for new) gur or jhola gur, the latter adjective indicating its similarity to jhol, the Bengali word for broth. In the markets it is sold in small earthen pitchers called nagris. For Bengalis, jhola gur has been immortalized in a nonsense poem written by Sukumar Ray, father of the great filmmaker Satyajit Ray. The poem enumerates the best things of life and declares that the best of the best is jhola gur poured over a slice of bread.

The second state of processing creates a grainy, sticky version that is equally delectable with homemade chapattis and commercially baked breads. Some people refer to it as nagri, because like the jhola gur, this too is sold in nagris. The third and final version of khejur gur is solid – formed into a disc called patali, about two to three inches in thickness and five to seven inches in diameter. It has a fudge-like consistency and melts in the mouth. Once the boiling mixture is judged to be ready, the gur maker pours it over a clean cloth draped over a line of shallow, rounded pits previously dug into a mound of soil. The weight of the gur makes the cloth sink into each of the pits, which serve as moulds for the patali gur. Once dried, the discs are easily removed from the cloth and wrapped up for sale. They can be stored in the refrigerator for almost a year – an attribute that Bengali expatriates all over the world take advantage of.

Throughout Bengal, both confectioners and home cooks eagerly anticipate winter, when they can switch from cane sugar to khejur gur. Over time, Bengalis have developed a wide variety of sweets known by the generic name of pitha, which are made with milk, wheat and rice flour, grated coconut and thickly evaporated milk. All of these are sweetened with khejur gur in winter, and it is no exaggeration to say than in areas noted for the quality of their date palms, the air is almost continuously infused with the redolence of khejur gur. Aside from pitha, one of Bengal's favourite home-made desserts is payesh or rice pudding. It has an aura of sanctity that makes it ideal for ritual offerings. Khejur gur significantly enhances the taste and flavour of payesh. From the late eighteenth century, cottage cheese or chhana became the prime material for confectioners, thus giving birth to the legendary Bengali rosogolla, sandesh, pantua, rajbhog, chamcham and many other sweets. Initially, cane sugar was the sweetener of choice for all of them. In the late nineteenth century, however, the confectioners of Nadia district in West Bengal began to experiment by using the freshly made khejur gur to sweeten sandesh. The product became wildly popular, and now it is hard to imagine a Bengali who does not yearn during the winter for this version of a beloved sweet – the whiteness of the chhana tinted browny beige, the delicate flavour of milk happily married to the distinctive essence of khejur gur.

It is not surprising that a product that generates such obsessive devotion should permeate the culture and ethos in ways beyond ingesting. Practitioners of Ayurvedic medicine swore by the health benefits of any kind of palm sugar, and modern medical research seems to support their claims. Khejur gur has a far lower glycemic index than cane sugar and also contains some essential minerals and vitamins. Residents of areas famed for the superior quality of their khejur gur take pride in bragging about it. The envious sometimes respond with a backhanded compliment, as in the jocular couplet describing the Bangladesh district of Faridpur as a place noted for its thieves, swindlers and khejur gur. Paintings and woodcuts often depict palm trees with clay pots suspended from their trunks. The Bauls, a community of roving minstrels whose songs are inspired by Sufi spirituality, often use the tapping of sap in a clay pot as a metaphor for their ritual practice of sexual retention. Bengali literature is replete with references to this magical ingredient. In a hilarious short story, Narayan Gangopadhyay describes a Bengali – justifiably proud of his khejur gur – offering a sample to a derisive British officer who shares a train compartment with him. The latter is so entranced by the delightful taste of this novelty that he tricks the Bengali into agreeing to an exchange; just before getting off the train, he takes the Bengali's entire stock of gur and leaves him with a package supposedly containing an assortment of the Englishman's favourite foods. Too late, the Bengali discovers that the package contains a large pumpkin.

Such stories were frequently told in my childhood home during winter when my father, a gur aficionado, scoured the market for both liquid and solid khejur gur. After each foray, he was the first one to taste the product with the solemn concentration that is normally seen only among tea and wine tasters. Once the verdict had been pronounced – and sometimes it could be a negative – the rest of us would happily indulge ourselves, regardless of the esoteric points of taste, consistency or flavour.

Even in today's globalized age, with restaurants providing the cuisines of many countries to city dwellers everywhere, khejur gur continues to be an obsession for Bengalis – ordinary consumers, discerning gourmets, confectioners. The culinary imagination refuses to rest on the laurels of the past. A prime example of this is the recent transformation of Bengal's second-most famous sweet, the rosogolla. Although sandesh, in winter, had been sweetened with khejur gur for more than a century, the rosogolla had not. During the past couple of decades, however, confectioners in Calcutta have boldly gone where no one has gone before, using a light syrup of khejur gur to immerse the rosogolla in winter. A shocking idea for traditionalists, this new version of rosogolla is a delightful revelation for the unprejudiced palate.

Even the professionals who specialize in solely making sandesh are coming up with newer ways to facilitate the marriage of chhana with khejur gur as is demonstrated by the products offered by some of Calcutta's best-known sweetshops. One named after the original proprietors, Girish Chandra Ghosh and Nakur Nandy, started in 1845 and is still flourishing. Behind glass cases filled with a variety of sandesh with alluring names, one can sense a hive of activity infused with flashes of genius. One of their concoctions is called monohora, literally 'that which steals your heart'. At first glance it is hard to think of this object with its smooth surface and deep brown color, as a true sandesh. Its texture and colour are totally alien to chhana. One bite, however, reveals the mystery. The soft, white chhana is completely encased in a firm shell of solid khejur gur, each element retaining its individuality, yet melting into a delectable union on the tongue. With every successive mouthful, the entranced consumer is only too happy to let her heart be stolen.

## Narkel Naru: an easy winter treat

### Process

Take a whole good-sized coconut, halve it and grate the flesh. In a large bowl, combine the grated coconut and granulated khejur gur, and gently knead the mixture. Taste to see if more gur is needed. Heat a pan or karai over medium heat and cook the coconut mixture, stirring constantly to prevent burning. In about ten or twelve minutes, the mixture will be cooked and emit the typical fragrance of coconut and khejur gur. Take the pan off the stove and start shaping the mixture into little balls (naru), using your hands. This has to be done while the mixture is still fairly hot, otherwise the coconut will fall apart. For those who wish to gild the lily, the basic coconut–khejur gur mixture can be enhanced with the addition of ground cardamom seeds, or even evaporated milk (kheer).

# Payesh

## Ingredients

*For four to six people:*

- 75 grams rice, preferably the Bengali Gobindabhog rice which is prized for its subtle fragrance and small grains
- 2 litres whole milk
- khejur gur broken into small pieces, about one cup
- 2 or 3 freshly ground cardamom pods (optional)

## Process

Rinse the rice in a colander and spread it out on a plate to dry. Stir occasionally, so that the rice dries evenly. Once it has dried, mix it with a teaspoon of ghee. This will prevent the rice from becoming sticky and forming clumps when it is being cooked.

Heat the milk in a pan that has been scrupulously

cleaned to remove any lingering odours of spices from previous cooking. Preferably, the pan for payesh or any other sweet should never be used for other kinds of cooking. Bring the milk to a boil over high heat and immediately reduce the flame to low. Keep stirring the milk so that it does not boil over, or stick to the bottom of the pan. This is a painstaking process and can take almost an hour until the milk has been reduced to 1.5 litres. Add the rice and again keep stirring until it is cooked. Make sure not to overcook, or the rice will turn into a mush. Now add the gur, a bit at a time, so that it is absorbed thoroughly. Taste and decide how sweet you want your payesh to be. Add the ground cardamom, if desired, and remove from the stove. In Bengali homes payesh is eaten either at room temperature or chilled.

# MAINS

# Tea with My Father

THE THIN, SINEWY LEGS EMERGING FROM THE FOLDS OF the dhoti made me think of a grasshopper. The owner of the legs stood on a wobbly stool and reached up to a wooden chest on the top shelf of his modest shop. The chest had a small, round opening with a fitted lid which the man removed and put in his pocket. In his left hand he had a steel bowl and a long iron hook which he inserted into the opening. With careful motions he drew out a portion of dark leaves that filled the bowl, put the lid back, and jumped down with surprising agility. As he held the bowl out to my father, the smile that bared his paan-stained teeth could only be described as beatific. From the lower elevation of a seven-year-old, I looked up and saw my father inhale deeply and hand the bowl back to the man. The smile on his face was no less beatific, though his teeth were far whiter.

'*Cholbey* (Will this do)?' asked Sarkar moshai from behind the counter.

'*Cholbey*,' said my father from the customer's side.

I had no idea of course of the deep appreciation for this particular tea conveyed by the deliberate understatement of 'cholbey'. It was the very first time I had gone with my father on one of his tea-purchasing expeditions, and the dim mystique of the store's interior, redolent of an unfamiliar scent, was what fascinated me, as did Sarkar moshai, lean as a hungry dog, keen as a hunting eagle as he assessed his customer's reaction. During my high school and college years, however, whenever I heard protesters marching on the streets of Calcutta, shouting '*cholchhey, cholbey*', or '*cholbey na, cholbey na*', I invariably went back to that little teashop.

My father had a love of the good things of life – food, music, poetry, conversation, movies – as everyone in our family knew. That he was also a man of limited means who showed little eagerness to pursue the acquisition of wealth puzzled people. Throughout his life he conducted himself as an aristocrat by temperament, and the lack of necessary means troubled him little. Tea – the expensive first or second flush harvests from estates in the Darjeeling area – was one luxury on which he spent large sums of money, often provoking irritated reactions from my mother. This was a dissonance that

I recognized from childhood. My parents were bonded by their love of good food and an overflowing impulse of hospitality. My mother was a renowned cook and my father was not only a discerning shopper but also a consumer with an exquisite palate. However, when it came to tea, a world of separation rose between them. My mother, who only started drinking tea when she was studying for her MA exams, found no merit in it except as an enabler of late-night wakefulness. She found the taste obnoxious, with or without milk and sugar. The only way she could drink it down was by adding lime juice to it. After their marriage, my father must have been dismayed to find his bride so lacking in appreciation for what he considered a glorious beverage. He bought the best tea he could get hold of, brewed it himself instead of letting any servant touch it, and looked hopefully at my mother as she took her first sips. Inevitably, as he told me in later years, her wrinkled nose and frowning forehead indicated his failure. After some time, he gave up on her. And she, having discovered in instant coffee an easy-to-make hot stimulant, was equally happy not to be subjected to his experiments. Ordinary, not-too-expensive tea was also used in our household. There were too many visitors of all kinds who had to be offered the obligatory cup and my mother occasionally had some with them, just to be polite. But her ingrained inability to appreciate a really superior cup of tea bred my father's determination to induct me into its rarefied pleasures – when the time was ripe.

Yes, time was an important factor. Like everybody in our extended family, he too believed that tea was not to be given to young children or even those in their early teens. I would have to wait until I was in college before I was allowed to have it. Others in the family, especially older female relatives, reinforced the ban by saying that tea had a ruinous effect on the livers of young people, and worse, that it darkened your skin – a mortal danger for a girl who had to face the marriage market. Still, there was no embargo on learning, and with that first expedition to Sarkar moshai's shop, my father started telling me about the many different varieties of a plant whose botanical name, *camellia sinensis*, carried an aura of exotic elegance. He described its roots in China and dispersal in India, Ceylon and Africa, its historical role in Buddhist cultures and, inevitably, he elaborated on the wiliness of the British in getting Indians addicted to tea through shrewd marketing. When I think back to those conversations after all these intervening decades, I am amazed at the depth and extent of his knowledge. In the days before Google, information was not at one's fingertips. Yet, as I have found, none of his stories were inaccurate. All of them filled me with an intense expectation of the time when I would be old enough to freely drink this marvellous beverage which had so much variety of flavour, colour and depth depending on origin, harvesting and processing, when terms like orange pekoe and pekoe would immediately tell me what a tea was like.

There were occasions when I did think of sneaking a sip, if I saw a half-filled teapot sitting ignored on a table. But the fear of being found out with a mouthful of hot liquid was a deterrent. That changed during one summer when a younger cousin from Delhi came to visit. Full of charm and energy, he was also mischief incarnate and talked me into reaching for forbidden pleasure. We chose an afternoon when the adults were either napping or engrossed in conversation far from the kitchen. After boiling some water, we poured it over a portion of tea leaves in the largest cup we could find. Somehow, the slow seeping of colour taking place before our eyes lacked the magic of transformation that happened invisibly in a teapot. To this day I believe my reluctance to use teabags in a cup stems from that incident. After staring at the liquid for what seemed an eternity, we each took a spoonful and sipped. Aside from the burning heat and a weird astringency, we tasted nothing.

'Milk and sugar?' said my cousin rather doubtfully.

'No, the milk is in the fridge – they'll hear us opening it,' I said.

With the gleam of sudden inspiration in his eyes, my cousin looked inside the kitchen cupboards, took out my mother's jar of instant coffee, and added a little bit to the tea.

'Now give it a taste,' he commanded.

'Taste,' I said, incensed. 'How can you expect me to taste this vile mixture?'

'Scientists always taste new things themselves,' he replied pompously. 'This will be my own creation – chaffee,' he replied and put a spoonful in his mouth.

The next moment, he choked and burst into a violent fit of coughing, splattering 'chaffee' all over the kitchen counter. The noise brought our mothers rushing to the kitchen and we had our ears boxed thoroughly. That was the end of my secret forays into tea tasting.

The day I learned I had secured admission to the English Department at Presidency College, my father declared it was time for a celebratory cup of tea. I felt I was being given the membership of an exclusive club as I sat at the dining table. Secretly, I was also afraid that after years of expectation, even the best available tea, brewed by a master like my father, would be a disappointment. I need not have worried. Being a purist, he first gave me a half cup without any milk or sugar. I bent forward to find my reflection in the pale golden liquid as the fragrance rose to my nostrils. I remembered my father inhaling the tea leaves in Sarkar moshai's teashop that was no longer in business. And I took my first sip. What a difference from the awful potation my cousin and I had created. It was a lesson in the value of deferred desires. I was given another portion with sugar and a third with both milk and sugar. Surprisingly, for a young and unsophisticated drinker, I preferred the version with sugar and no milk.

My mother, watching us with fond exasperation, said she was glad that I was rejecting the combination of milk with tea, just the way she had. My father gave her a look, but wisely said nothing. Instead, he reminded me that run-of-the-mill teas were better with the addition of milk and sugar. I had no trouble believing that. The roadside tea stalls, serving cheap tea, did not allow for individual preferences. Their tea was brewed together with milk and sugar. And I was sure that many people preferred that to the thin, delicate, aromatic liquid my father loved. A great example was the pundit who used to give me home tutorials in Sanskrit before my final school-leaving exams. He had only two visible teeth and every time my mother brought him a cup of tea, sweetened with extra sugar as per his request, he asked for some muri (puffed rice). Taking a handful of muri, he dropped it into the cup and took a gigantic slurp that conveyed the floating muri and a large amount of tea into his mouth. The sequence was repeated until the muri and the tea had been consumed. Each time he put his cup down and reached for the next portion of muri, I took a good look at the remaining tea, but never did I find a single leftover grain of muri in it. He had developed his art of suction to perfection, but he had no palate.

Going to college changed my world and my habits. Suddenly, I was freed from the restrictions and tight supervision of school life. The hour-long commute by tram or bus to and from my home in south Calcutta meant my parents could not demand my return by a stipulated time. College Street, where Presidency College was located, hummed with a dynamic liveliness. The sidewalk stalls selling second-hand books and foreign magazines, the 'proper' bookstores staffed by arrogant yet knowledgeable men who seemed curiously reluctant to sell their volumes, the milling crowd of students, teachers, office workers and vendors of street food – all added up to an atmosphere of exuberant contention. And most wonderful of all was the luring portal of Coffee House, an institution almost as venerable and irresistible as the college itself.

It was at Coffee House that I first learned to savour the pleasures of coffee, especially the hitherto unknown 'cold coffee', or 'cold coffee with cream', which came in tall glasses. My friends, like me, had little pocket money. We dealt with that by asking for three or four straws which we dipped in the single glass we ordered and took turns in sipping the liquid that invested us with an aura of foreign sophistication. All around us, the tables were abuzz with loud conversation, mostly focusing on leftist ideas – an internal reflection of the '*cholbey na, cholbey na*' that was heard so often on the streets. This was the Calcutta of the sixties when the Naxalite movement was at its peak. As we were to discover later, even institutions like Presidency were not immune to the violent disruptions created by the movement. Although politics aroused little interest in me, the charged atmosphere of Coffee House brought a new kind of excitement to my life. I found the place addictive and spent too many hours there when I should have been attending classes.

This, naturally, was something I assiduously concealed at home. With the typical innocence of loving parents, mine imagined their only child to be solely immersed in the scholarly regimen of an elite institution. At home, on weekends, my father and I enjoyed our tea rituals. Occasionally, he would tell me about discovering a different tea store that sold interesting new varieties as well as old favourites. I knew better than to tell him about my new-found pleasure in drinking coffee.

When I left Calcutta to study at Harvard, my parents were both proud and sad. In the bustle of preparing for the momentous journey, I missed many occasions of having a leisurely cup of tea with my father. And I wondered whether in America I would become a coffee drinker and lose my palate for tea. I need not have worried. One of the big disappointments in America was the kind of coffee I encountered – strong and bitter, a world apart from the chicory-flavoured milky Indian coffee I knew. The tea was an even greater disappointment. In those days, the American public had not woken to the pleasures of fine teas, and all we could have was a tasteless liquid brewed with teabags.

As the months passed, I had other things on my mind besides the lack of good tea. I fell in love with a fellow student who was considered absolutely unacceptable as a husband by the standards of our society. Despite the violent objections of my family, and after months and months of furious argument by mail, we ended up getting married. After that, my father stopped writing to me. My mother, broken-hearted though she was, continued. Thankfully, my parents loved me too much to ever think of disowning me. Eventually, when I told them I was returning home for a visit, and that they would have the opportunity to meet my husband and see that he was not at all different from any of the 'acceptable' men I had been expected to marry, they must have been petrified. Not only was there the concern about how relatives and neighbours would behave, they probably quaked at the prospect of how they themselves would react to the outsider.

I chose to go alone first, hoping to mend bridges and ease the way for the problematic son-in-law. When I stepped out of the airport customs area, my heart beat fast and my throat felt dry. My parents had come with one of my aunts. The three middle-aged figures stood there, straight and stiff, bracing themselves for the encounter with the prodigal child. I looked first at my aunt. She gave me an awkward smile that was almost a grimace. My mother – a mother more than anything else – gave me a look of so much love and joy that I felt the anxiety ebb from my body. Finally, I looked at my father. He refused to meet my eyes, although a slight bending of his lips indicated an effort at a smile. My body tensed again as I moved forward.

We got home at lunchtime. My mother had made several of my favourite items. Throughout the meal, my aunt kept up an endless patter about relatives, neighbours, friends and the inequities of the government – a well-meaning effort to bridge the silence that extended from my father to me. I ate the delicious meal as if it was a penance and wondered what would happen at tea time. I imagined my aunt or my mother bustling around to make tea and felt I would not be able to swallow a drop.

I had reckoned without the love of a father. Late in the afternoon, he finally looked at me. It was not a look of anger or blame. It was the look of a parent who knows that forgiving a child is more necessary to him than to the child, even though he feels bewildered by the depth of the child's betrayal.

'I've found a new store near Gariahat market,' he said. 'They stock some really good teas. I've been trying them out over the last few days. I believe I know which one you'll like best.'

He rose to go to the kitchen. I felt the tears in my eyes, the lump in my throat. But I willed them away and gave him the biggest, brightest smile I could.

## Chirar Polau: a tasty and nutritious accompaniment to afternoon tea

### Ingredients

*For three or four people:*

- 250 grams chira (parched rice/poha)
- 2 medium potatoes
- a small head of cauliflower
- 120 grams shelled green peas
- 6 tablespoons mustard oil
- 2 sticks of cinnamon
- 3 whole cardamoms
- 3 cloves
- 2 or 3 green chillies
- 1 teaspoon posto (poppy seeds)
- salt to taste
- kari leaves for garnishing (optional)

## Process

Discard any impurities in the chira, wash in a colander by pouring hot water over it several times, and leave covered until the softened chira becomes dry and fluffy. Peel the potatoes and cut them into tiny cubes. Cut the cauliflower into tiny florets, discarding the hard central stem. Steam the peas for a few minutes. Heat 6 tablespoons of oil in a pan and fry the potatoes and cauliflower until brown and set aside. Add the whole spices, chillies and posto to the oil and then add the dried chira and steamed peas. Fry for about 2 or 3 minutes before adding the potatoes and cauliflower. Add some salt and fry for about 5 or 6 minutes before removing from the stove. Garnish with kari leaves if you wish, and serve immediately with hot cups of tea.

# Dining on Faith

THE HEADLINE IN *THE STATESMAN* STARED AT ME. BIG, bold and black, the two-inch letters proclaimed 'Bangladesh Declares Independence'.

It was 27 March 1971. In the dining room of their Calcutta house, my parents and I silently looked at one another before gazing again at those ominous letters. The same thought, I knew, haunted each of us. This headline was not just history in the making; it could also spell tragedy for me.

The political convulsion in Bangladesh (formerly East Pakistan) and its violent consequences entered deeply into my personal life because of my marriage, in 1968, to a Bengali Muslim from that region. We had met as graduate students at Harvard. When I announced that I intended to marry him, my orthodox Hindu Brahmin family was horrified. I had been the first girl in our family allowed to go abroad for higher education, alone and unmarried. Everyone now regretted it. In a family where even inter-caste marriages raised eyebrows, marrying a Muslim would bring unbearable social stigma. Worse, the Muslim I wanted to marry was a citizen of Pakistan, a country hostile to India. If war broke out, I might be cut off from my parents. And since Muslims could have four wives, what if this young man had one or more tucked away back home?

Would I be forced to convert to Islam, they asked. The gods must have shuddered at the prospect. Eating beef, usually forbidden to Hindus, is common among Muslims. Would my palate, too, be so defiled? The mere possibility seemed to cast a shadow of pollution over the daily offerings set before the family gods.

Despite all objections, we got married in the dusty offices of an American justice of the peace. My husband was a non-believer. His family at home consisted of older married siblings, all of whom appeared thrilled at the prospect of meeting their baby brother's exotic wife. None expected me to convert. On my side, after an appalled and deafening silence, we received a reluctant acceptance of the marriage from my parents. But my devout grandmother amazed me with a letter of joyful congratulations, unmarred by misgivings about our future.

We left the US in October 1970. After meeting my

in-laws and spending a month with them in Dhaka, I went to Calcutta alone – the remorseful daughter in search of forgiveness and love. I think by the time my first delectable meal at home was over – my favourite items lovingly cooked by my mother – much of the hurt had been set aside. I was to stay for three months, while my husband joined his office in Dhaka and found an apartment. But before he could come and meet my parents, political events overtook us. Normal travel between Calcutta and Dhaka became impossible. And then came the declaration of independence.

For three nights and four days, we had no news of my husband. The papers reported on the terror unleashed by the Pakistani military, especially its systematic elimination of Bengali intellectuals – such as my husband. We also knew that his marriage to a Hindu woman from enemy India made him even more of a target for reprisal.

Panic-stricken refugees streamed across the border into Calcutta. Train stations were jam-packed with huddled figures. Newspaper photos showed people hunkering over bowls containing pathetic handfuls of rice. Our house became deathly quiet – my father and I remaining glued to newspapers and radio but afraid to discuss anything we heard, my mother seeking haven with the gods in her worshipping room.

When my husband turned up on the fourth evening, after an escape across the Comilla–Agartala border and a two-day train journey, my parents welcomed him with unrestrained joy and relief. No shadow of resentment and suspicion towards the Muslim son-in-law was evident. Their only daughter was not a widow – that was all they cared about.

My mother cheerfully bustled around in the kitchen, fixing an impromptu dinner. Oppressed by fear in the past few days, we had neglected to shop, and our larder and refrigerator were almost bare. But her culinary genius transcended such limitations.

Later, I watched my husband eat his first meal in our house. Instead of rice, my mother served luchis – puffy, disc-shaped fried breads that Bengalis love. As he picked up the first luchi and punctured the top layer with his finger to let out the hot, fragrant air, a smile of almost childlike pleasure illuminated his face, erasing the tensions of his traumatic journey. When I saw that smile mirrored on my parents' faces, I began to hope that he would really become the son they never had.

The luchis came with eggplant fritters, a tangy potato dish, a dal made from yellow split peas, and a chilled dessert of evaporated milk infused with tangerine pulp. Afterwards, we decided to walk to my widowed grandmother's house and give her the good news in person. She was eating her solitary supper but came out when she heard my voice. The instant she saw my husband, she rushed forward and hugged him tightly, unaware that her hand, smeared with the spiced vegetables she had been eating with chapatis, left turmeric-yellow fingerprints on his white silk kurta. The signature of true love, I thought.

The honeymoon, however, was brief. Being a penniless, statusless refugee in his in-laws' home seemed to bring out the most prickly and acerbic aspects of my husband's character. Those traits collided head on with my mother's natural propensity to impose her way of doing things – even on people accustomed to independence from an early age. The 'house rules', which I no longer noticed because I had grown up with them, were numerous and intrusive. No breakfast until you had eaten a morsel of the offerings made to the gods during morning worship. No leaving the house without putting one grain of the 'holy rice' (from the Jagannatha Temple in Puri) in your mouth. My husband, who never fasted during Ramadan as his fellow Muslims did, who never went to a mosque to pray, found it absurd and irritating to be subjected to these Hindu rituals.

Worst of all were the daily (and befuddling) restrictions stemming from the purity code known as 'enthho'. Derived from the Sanskrit uchhishtho, enthho has become an amorphous term for Bengali Hindus, its interpretation varying from family to family. Anything that has touched your mouth or saliva becomes enthho. Observant Hindus will never bite into a fruit or sip from a glass and then offer the rest to someone else. The term becomes more puzzling, however, when applied to rice, which is not enthho when uncooked but becomes so after cooking. Once you have touched anything containing cooked rice, you must wash your hands before touching uncooked vegetables, fruits, spices or even clean containers. The status of animal products – fish, meat, eggs – is less confusing. They are always enthho, cooked or uncooked. A bowl of cooked vegetables is not enthho and can be placed anywhere; but the minute the bowl comes into contact with anything containing cooked rice, it becomes enthho and can only be kept in an area (dining table, kitchen counter, refrigerator shelf) set aside for enthho foods.

The same rule applies to one's hands. When my husband, after sitting down for a meal, got up and opened the refrigerator to get iced water, he precipitated a crisis of pollution. For though he had not actually used his hand to eat, he had touched the plate containing rice and other foods. The refrigerator was immediately emptied of its contents, its interior washed thoroughly, and holy water from the Ganges (always stored in a small jar in the worship room) sprinkled over it for final purification. Naturally, my husband's comments about the meaninglessness of such practices did nothing to endear him to my mother. Later, I heard her lamenting to a visiting cousin about his refusal to learn the rituals of good health and purity.

No such reservations about non-believers, however, affected her response to some of my husband's friends who also had fled the ravages of the Pakistani soldiery. Both she and my father saw these young men as true refugees, since they were roughing it in the Bangladeshi Embassy. Expectations of conduct or conformity did not intrude between my mother and these visitors, whom she pampered with numerous Bengali delicacies. One of them often got his favourite dish – puishaak (a spinach-like leafy green) with tiny shrimp, ground mustard and green chillies. Watching her undiluted delight in feeding him, I wished things could have stayed that way between her and my husband.

May is one of the hottest months in Bengal. The mercury climbs into the nineties and refuses to budge. The sun blazes from a merciless blue sky. And while the cracked earth, melting asphalt and wizened leaves on the trees might create an illusion of desert-like aridity, the air is laden with a sullen moisture that drains one of all energy. May 1971 stands out in my memory as a relentless inferno.

The second month of the Bengali calendar, Jaishtha, runs from mid-May to mid-June. Every Tuesday in Jaishtha, married women observe a midday ritual – eating only uncooked rice flakes with yoghurt and fruit, while men and unmarried women eat the normal foods. My mother insisted I join her in this practice. I agreed to, despite my husband's jibes about reverting to the Dark Ages. But one Tuesday, when he offered me a spoonful from his potatoes delectably mashed with mustard oil, fried onions and fried chillies (a dish I loved), I could not resist. Convinced the gods would punish me for such transgression, my mother furiously gave vent to her frustrations, which were further exacerbated when, instead of showing contrition, my husband simply ignored her.

After this, I wondered what she planned for the most important ritual of Jaishtha – Jamaishashthi, when a Bengali mother-in-law prepares an elaborate midday feast for her son-in-law. The rationale (in a society where a woman's dependence on her husband was absolute) was that if he felt fussed over, he would treat his wife with care and affection. Would my mother choose not to do anything special for a son-in-law who showed so little consideration for all that was meaningful to her?

When the day arrived, I saw my fears had been groundless. My father was dispatched early to shop for a feast. When he returned, I rushed into the kitchen. The first thing I noticed was a huge head of rui (Bengal's favourite carp). This is an obligatory part of the son-in-law's feast. My mother would make a murighanto – a dry, spicy dish in which fried pieces of fish head are combined with diced potatoes and grains of atap (non-parboiled) rice. A paste of cinnamon, cardamom and cloves blends with the fish brain to create a unique redolence.

Looking around, I realized that my mother had planned the menu specifically to please my husband. For starters, she would serve kalmi shaak (water spinach), stir-fried with chopped garlic, dried chillies and the spice mixture called panch phoron. Eggplant fritters and a dal made with roasted moong beans would come next, followed by two vegetable items: stems of kochu (a kind of taro) cooked with ground mustard, fresh-ground coconut and small shrimp; and a dish of banana blossom. Next came the carp head, followed by two Bengali specialties – prawn malaikari (made with clarified butter, coconut milk and spices) and chitol in a fiery red-chilli sauce.

This last item astonished me. We had never eaten chitol when I was growing up. It was a 'difficult' fish – very bony in the back, very oily in the stomach – generally favoured by the people of eastern Bengal.

Later, my mother had learned from a friend from the area how to make fish balls with the bony flesh. Today she was ready to tackle the chitol because my husband loved it.

My offers of help were imperiously waved away. This was one meal she was going to prepare all by herself – a gift from mother-in-law to son-in-law. The heat of the June day mounted, carrying the rich, mingled aromas of cooking, but I felt oppressed at the thought of her being locked in the steamy kitchen. When a couple of my husband's friends showed up and suggested going out for coffee, I decided to stay home in case my mother did need help. She did not. By one-thirty, she was done – an amazing feat.

Bathed and refreshed, she laid the table, expecting my husband to return soon. My father, himself an epicure, happily talked about the Jamaishashthi meals he had eaten in the early years of their marriage. I peeked at all the dishes and repeatedly inhaled the fragrance of each, as I had done in childhood. But there was no sign of the guest of honour. When he did return, around two-thirty, he said he had eaten some snacks with his coffee and was not hungry. He would skip lunch. We should go ahead and eat, he said.

I am sure he had no idea of the magnitude of the affront. Of how unthinkable it was for a mother-in-law to eat on Jamaishashthi while her son-in-law remained unfed. But even I was taken aback at the intensity of my mother's reaction. She shut herself in her bedroom, sobbed loudly and launched into a monologue that was part tirade, part dirge. Never had she been so humiliated. For what sins were the gods punishing her? And how could her only beloved daughter have married a man so utterly disrespectful to her?

For an eternity, no one tried to stop her. My father, my husband and I – each in a different room – listened in stricken silence. Eventually, my father intervened. Though he had a sneaking sympathy for my husband, he persuaded him to offer an apology, however much it went against the grain. My husband, too, had begun to realize how deep was the hurt. Sadly, he knocked on her door to express penitence.

Much later that day, my father and I ate a little bit of the glorious meal my mother had prepared. Afterwards, I convinced her to have a tiny mouthful and drink some water, using the argument that her anger, sorrow and fasting would simply bring bad luck to my husband, which was sure to affect me. This was an argument she couldn't resist.

In the evening, she finally served the Jamaishashthi feast to the intended recipient. My father and I sat and watched anxiously. The meal began in a constrained silence. But with every mouthful the magic of her cooking worked wonders. My husband's compliments were effusive and completely spontaneous. When he was finally served the chitol, he looked up at her and smiled with delight. She smiled back. At last, my father and I could relax.

At the end of July, my husband received a fellowship that enabled us to return to the US. When they said goodbye, I was astonished by the frankness with which they asked each other to pardon their mutual lack of understanding. During all subsequent visits, the two of them always treated each other with deep affection and respect – feelings that remained unchanged even after my divorce.

# Chitol Kopta

## Ingredients

*For the koptas:*

- 500 grams chitol fish (the back portion)
- 2 medium potatoes, boiled and mashed
- ½ teaspoon ginger paste
- 1 medium onion finely chopped
- 1 beaten egg
- mustard oil
- salt to taste
- a small handful of freshly chopped mint leaves (optional)

*For the sauce:*

- 2 medium onions finely chopped
- ½ teaspoon ginger paste
- ½ teaspoon turmeric powder

- 1 teaspoon chilli powder
- 2 bay leaves
- 3 one-inch pieces of cinnamon
- 4 cardamoms
- 4 cloves
- ½ cup mustard oil
- salt and sugar to taste

## Process

First scoop out the fish from the skin with a spoon, carefully moving the spoon the way the bones are laid. If the spoon moves against them, the bones will come away with the fish. Combine the fish with the mashed potatoes, salt, ginger, onion, beaten egg and chopped mint if desired. Knead gently to form a tight dough-like lump. Divide it into little round or oval balls, patting each smooth between wet palms. Heat about half a cup of mustard oil and deep-fry the fish balls in it. In the hot oil, they will swell up like little balloons, though they will shrink later, when removed from the pan. The mashed potato adds a nice fluffiness to the texture of the fish balls. These koptas can be served by themselves as a snack or appetizer, or an item to have with rice and dal.

Usually, however, they are cooked in a sauce and served with rice. Heat the oil remaining in the pan (adding some more, if necessary) and add the bay leaves, cinnamon, cardamom and cloves. Fry for a couple of minutes before adding the onion and fry until golden brown. Add a little sugar to caramelize the onion. Add all the other spices and fry them well. Add a cup and a half of water (or more if required later), some salt and bring to a boil. Add the fish koptas and cook covered for five or six minutes. Taste for salt and sugar balance, and remove from the stove.

# Green Noodles by the River

I FIRST WENT TO SADARGHAT, DHAKA'S BIGGEST RIVER terminal, in the spring of 1974. I was about to embark on my first trip by steamer from Dhaka to Barisal. Standing on the pier, looking around eagerly while waiting to board, my eyes fell on what seemed like a heap of pale green noodles. Appearance, however, was not reality. A cucumber had been artfully transformed by a young man in a food vendor's stall.

Sadarghat milled with a truculent energy, to which a babel of dialects, all Bengali, yet frequently unintelligible, gave voice. The occasional bleating of a goat or the clucking of chickens added to the cacophony. Steamboats loomed over us from their moorings. Farther away bobbed smaller fishing boats pinpointed by the diminutive beams of lanterns and oil lamps. Fumes of diesel and kerosene infused the air along with the odours of organic refuse, fried fish, chilli pepper, garlic, onion and spiced meats. The commercial pulse of the city throbbed around me.

To my Calcutta Hindu family, Dhaka had always been a remote watery hinterland teeming with Muslims – a place of unimaginable perils best left unexplored. When I announced I was going to live there, several years after I shocked them by marrying a Bangladeshi Muslim, they gave me up for lost. They could not understand why we did not find a way to stay on in America. My own expectations of living in the newly independent country were more optimistic, tinged only slightly with trepidation.

It didn't take long to discover that under the legible surface of a shared Bengali culture and language lay the more abstruse narrative of a city still married to the village. The long-drawn shriek of a lone white-breasted kite flying over the river carried enigmatic messages from distant zones, quite unlike the banal cawing of crows in Calcutta. Instead of high-rises, lakes filled with fish and enormous shade trees modified the cityscape, as did the banana groves and climbing vines around many houses.

Dhaka was the capital of a country that had staked its existence on being Bengali. For me, the Bengali from across the border, it presented a delightfully different expression of that identity, whether in the city's euphoric celebration of the Bengali New Year, or during festivals when folksy touches coloured the exotic and the Islamic. Eating the same vegetables, dal and fish I had grown up with, I was initially baffled by an unfamiliar undertaste, until I discovered the ubiquity of onions in the cuisine. Bengal's glorious fish, hilsa, became more than a mere accompaniment for rice. Baked into a rice-flour crepe, it stunned my palate with its delicate intensity. And at elaborate formal banquets, I occasionally came across the cucumber-as-noodles I had first seen in Sadarghat.

When I turned up for the preliminary ceremonies at a friend's wedding, I was scolded by his mother for not wearing a yellow sari, the appropriate clothing for the 'turmeric' ritual. Until then, I had no idea that this ritual, an inextricable part of Bengali Hindu weddings, could have any role in the contractual marriage ceremony of Muslims. Even nature presented a richer aspect. I learned to see the monsoon, Bengal's signature season, as a deep, dark, joyous phenomenon, not merely an urban inconvenience.

Yet, the longer I lived in Dhaka, the more I found the charming otherness of the place invaded by disquieting, ominous elements – personal, social and political. Distrustful, impertinent queries from strangers deepened my unease: 'From India? Hindu?' they asked, their narrowed eyes filled with unfriendly surmise –

something that had never occurred in the early years of my stay. One day, hearing the daily prayer calls, I found myself aching for the sound of conch shells or temple bells, accompaniments of Hindu rituals I had never cared for earlier. Fine cracks – no more than the width of a consonant here, a vowel there – began to jolt my new-found relationships, leaving me desperately seeking a better vocabulary. The place I had once embraced as a home seemed increasingly alien. Dhaka, itself losing its modest charms en route to becoming a megacity, was making me into a foreigner rather than a Bengali.

In the absurd comedic course of life, the mantle of otherness even wrapped itself around me, as when a part-time maid reported how she had vigorously defended my reputation on hearing my neighbour remark I was a Hindu from India. After all, how could a person like me, who treated her servants so kindly, be anything but a genuine, god-fearing Muslim woman? Not having the courage to disillusion her, I held my peace, but the tiny act of self-negation left its mark. Along with several others, it propelled me to a point where optimism about making an acceptable life was finally vanquished. Still, it was not easy to turn away. The riverine soul of the city had secretly seeped into mine, and the sorrow of departure overwhelmed me like a monsoon flood.

Distanced now from the upheaval of that life, I feel relief and regret. Sometimes, I find myself back in Sadarghat. Under the sweeping indigo wings of a spring evening, the Buriganga River is a field of silvery grey. I see the young man with the cucumber, focused as a yogi, fingers plying his transforming knife. Among the many aspirations, big and small, I left unfulfilled in Dhaka is learning how to turn a cucumber into a plateful of green noodles.

## Kadam Bhai's Duck Bhuna

Kadam Bhai was a family friend from Barisal. He made this dish when I visited his home in the village of Dapdapia.

### Ingredients

- a nice, plump duck, skinned, cleaned and cut into 12–13 portions – 2 drumsticks, 2 thighs, 2 wings, 4 breast pieces and assorted pieces from the rest (discard the giblets)
- 120 grams onion paste
- 1 tablespoon ginger paste
- 2 teaspoons each of garlic paste, chilli, turmeric, cumin and coriander powder
- whole spices consisting of 3 one-inch pieces of cinnamon, ¼ teaspoon of ground black pepper and 2 bay leaves

- 2 small onions and 6–7 large garlic cloves finely chopped
- 10–12 whole peppercorns
- 5 tablespoons mustard oil
- 2 tablespoons ghee
- half a cup of water
- salt

## Process

Mix the pieces of duck thoroughly with all the ground and pasted spices, as well as the cinnamon and bay leaves, mustard oil and water, and cook, tightly covered, over a low flame until the meat is absolutely tender. Shake the pot from time to time so that the contents do not stick to the bottom. Remove from the fire and set aside. In a separate pot, heat the ghee, add the peppercorns, chopped onion and garlic and fry until golden brown. Add the cooked duck pieces and stir thoroughly for 4 to 5 minutes until no moisture is left and the sheen of oil is visible. Check for salt and remove from the stove.

This dry preparation can be served with either Bengali khichuri or parota. The best accompaniment, if you can make it, would be green cucumber noodles.

# Seeds of Dreams

THE LATE APRIL AFTERNOON GLOWERED WITH HEAT. Most of the slatted window shutters of our house in Calcutta were closed to keep the interior as cool as possible. But with the kitchen windows left open for ventilation, we were not totally immune to the sounds and aromas of life from the street, backyard and surrounding houses. And there it was again – the characteristic rumbling sound of something heavy being dragged across a concrete floor. Moments later came the resonance of stone grating on stone.

My father and I looked at each other and grinned. We knew what it meant. Our next-door neighbour was entertaining yet another guest from his home village in Rarh, the westernmost corner of West Bengal. And no matter what hour of day or time of year it was, lunch or dinner in that house was unthinkable without a fresh-ground serving of posto, the tiny white seeds of the Indian opium poppy.

Ground posto was prepared in our house as well. The shil, a flat block of roughly pitted stone, and the nora, a heavy pestle-shaped bar of stone – standard equipment in all Bengali kitchens – were used every day to grind, paste and powder any number of ingredients. As a child, I loved to squat beside our maid on summer mornings and watch her crush the pale poppy seeds with several sprinklings of water until she had produced a smooth, round, beige-coloured mass. If I brought my face down close to it, I could smell its delicate, almost herbal fragrance, like wet grass on a hot summer day after the first rainfall; I inhaled again and again to absorb its freshness.

The relationship between food and the seasons was a matter of deep conviction in my family. During the summer we tended to eat 'cold' foods which, according to Bengali food lore, were easy on the stomach and kept the body cool. 'Hot' items like onion, garlic, eggs and meat supposedly inflamed the body, so we avoided them until autumn and winter. Posto, itself a cool ingredient, was frequently added to cool vegetables. One summer favourite was jhingey, a courgette-like vegetable, combined with cubed potatoes and seasoned with nigella seeds, green chillies, and ground posto. Eggplant or potatoes by themselves were also cooked with ground posto. My widowed grandmother, a vegetarian, was particularly fond of posto fritters, hot and crisp, eaten as a starter with rice and dal. Sometimes, on a cool, damp monsoon afternoon, my mother made the fritters as a savoury snack that we ate at teatime.

It was not until years later, when I was in college, that I first heard about the other product of the poppy plant and its role in our family. It came out almost casually that my mother's grandmother regularly took opium in the last years of her life. What I found more shocking than the fact itself was how calmly the adults accepted it. Apparently, the habit was common among elderly people of my great-grandmother's generation, like taking snuff or chewing tobacco, and carried no stigma. A daily opium pill simply guaranteed relief from the aches, pains and infirmities of old age.

My mother – with her small, delicate child's fingers – was entrusted with the task of rolling the dark, gummy raw opium into tiny balls, which were then stored in a little silver box. Afterwards, she would hold her hand to her nose to inhale the subtle aroma. In the evenings, she often sat by her grandmother and watched her pop an opium pill and then drink a cup of warm milk. As the drug slowly took effect, my great-grandmother (who was also a devotee of posto dishes) launched into stories and reminiscences until she fell asleep.

The opium poppy, *Papaver somniferum*, has been part of human history for centuries. The latex from the unripe seedpods yields opium and its derivatives, but the tiny kidney-shaped seeds have minimal narcotic effect because they form after the seedpods have ripened. Native to western Asia and southeastern Europe, the plant has been cultivated on the Indian subcontinent as a source of opium since the eleventh and twelfth centuries, when Arab traders, who learned about opium from the Greeks, brought the knowledge to India.

In 1757, the last nawab of Bengal was dethroned by the British East India Company, which subsequently concentrated on maximizing the cultivation of opium in Bengal. The drug promised to generate huge profits, not only in the local market, but also in a far bigger one – China. The company's greed was so great that at one point they forced farmers in much of Bengal to devote all their arable land to its cultivation. So it's not surprising that the posto seeds produced in this enormous poppy-growing zone became such an important element in the local diet.

The Indian trade in opium flourished unimpeded until the 1820s, when Chinese emperor Tao-kuang tried to restrict imports. The British, unwilling to surrender their lucrative trade, fought back. When the Chinese lost the Second Opium War, in 1858, they responded by legalizing opium cultivation and knocking the bottom out of the Bengali market.

But while the Indian opium trade may have diminished, the local taste for posto did not. I discovered this during a recent visit to my father's hometown in the Rarh area, a journey I had been meaning to make since his death in 1993.

The moment I got off the train, a shield of fire seemed to rise out of the earth and hit me. No wonder, I thought, that the people of this region were so addicted to posto, the magical ingredient they believed would dispel the debilitating effect of such heat.

As the heat abated with the setting sun, I walked down a road bordered by tall palash trees, their vivid orange flowers, shaped like the beaks of parrots, blazing on dark branches. I was going to Subarnarekha, a bookstore in the university town of Shantiniketan that is the daily gathering place for an eclectic and intellectual crowd. The mention of posto created a visible stir. Like our neighbour in Calcutta so many years ago, people here consider posto integral to a meal, spending up to a quarter of their food budget to buy it. The poor use it sparingly, as a condiment. The better-off use it in a variety of sophisticated preparations, including one I had never heard of – a tart and zesty chutney with tamarind. An elderly woman buying a book of patterns for batik-printed silk told me that when her husband developed heart trouble, the local doctor advised him to eat more posto; supposedly, it lowered one's cholesterol. Myth and modern medicine – the local passion for posto seemed to have combined the two.

When I returned to the States, I tried to describe my visit to my mother. I told her that now that I had seen the region where my father grew up, I could visualize some of his childhood. I noticed after this that she began to start talking more frequently about my father, particularly his favourite dishes. One cold evening in March, as snow covered the ground and daylight faded rapidly, I stood looking out of the window, yearning for light, sun and colour. Rarh, with its red soil exhaling a fiery breath, seemed as distant and unreachable as Mars, as irretrievable as my father's presence. An overwhelming desire possessed me – a yearning to somehow capture its warmth and bring it into this cold white world. I decided I would make ground posto, seasoned with mustard oil, salt and chillies, and serve it as a starter with rice.

I turned away from the window and told my mother about my dinner plan. She smiled with pleasurable anticipation. Letting the posto soak in a bowl of warm water before grinding it by hand, I came and sat down beside her. Once again, she started reminiscing about how much my father had loved all the dishes she made with this ingredient – potatoes floating in a thin gravy of ground posto enlivened with slit green chillies; eggplant or jhingey flavoured with whole nigella seeds and coated with the beige-brown sauce of ground posto; hot, crisp fritters made with coconut, posto and rice flour, served with fragrant Darjeeling tea.

As she talked, I picked up one of her hands and looked at the fingers. No longer tender and delicate but roughened with age and work, these were the fingers that had once, long ago, rolled tiny balls of opium. We sat together, our fingers interleaved, while my mother's voice led me deeper and deeper into the sunny, tropical terrain of our mutual past. On my kitchen counter, the posto slowly softened in its watery bath.

## Posto Bata

Eaten with hot rice as a starter for the midday meal, almost like a relish, posto bata is the simplest way to enjoy the delicate yet addictive taste of Indian poppy seeds. It is eaten more commonly in West Bengal than in the east and many Bengalis believe that the posto grown in Bengal tastes better than that in any other part of India.

### Process

Take 50 grams of posto and soak it in water for half an hour. The traditional practice is to drain the posto and then grind it to a smooth paste on the grinding stone. Modern cooks, however, can grind the posto in a blender or a mixer, though the consistency will not be as perfect as that achieved through stone-grinding – smooth, yet not watery. Once the posto has been ground, mix it with salt, fresh mustard oil and chopped green chillies, all according to individual preference.

# Lamb with Posto

## Ingredients

*For four people:*

- 1 kilogram bone-in lamb, cut into pieces
- 2 large onions
- a 2-inch-long piece of fresh ginger
- an entire head of garlic (small size), chopped as finely as possible
- 4–5 one-inch pieces of cinnamon
- 6 whole cardamom pods
- 4 bay leaves
- 6–7 whole dry chillies
- 50 grams whole posto soaked in water
- ½ cup ghee
- salt (start with 1 teaspoon)
- 3 teaspoons sugar

## Process

Wash and clean the lamb. Heat ghee over medium heat in a thick-bottomed pan and add the cinnamon, cardamom and bay leaves. After frying them a couple of minutes, add the onion, ginger and garlic and fry until brown. Add the meat, salt and sugar and keep stirring until the meat becomes dark brown. Add the posto and the dry red chillies. Add enough hot water to cover the meat, cover the pan tightly and leave on a low flame until the meat is absolutely tender. Check from time to time to make sure it doesn't stick to the bottom. When the meat is done, uncover and finish the dish over a high flame, stirring vigorously until all the water has evaporated. Taste for salt and sugar – the sweetness should be pronounced. Although there are no ground spices, the presence of the chillies provides piquancy and the minute graininess of the posto counters the tenderness of the meat very well.

# A Shared Plate

'THE TATTO IS HERE, THE TATTO IS HERE!'

Bare feet rush down the stairs and out towards the front door as the house resonates with the blowing of conch shells and loud ululation – auspicious sounds believed to scare away evil spirits.

Staying with a friend in Calcutta to attend her daughter's wedding, I am caught up in the prevailing excitement. The tatto whose arrival is causing such a commotion is a collection of gifts – clothes, cosmetics, decorative objects, food – that the bridegroom's family sends to the home of the bride on the morning of a Bengali Hindu wedding. I haven't attended such an event in many years, but my memory flashes to long-forgotten images of the gifts sent to our house for an aunt's wedding. As a small child, I had been particularly awed by one item – an enormous carp, its silvery scales gleaming with an undertone of pink, its head patterned with turmeric and vermilion, a double garland of tuberoses twined round its ample belly. Is such a princely fish still part of the Bengali wedding tatto?

I move forward to look at the trays being unloaded from the car. Yes, one does contain a carp, although its dimensions fall short of those I remember. But the family seems pleased, to judge from their gleeful comments about the muror dal to be made with the head at lunchtime. For us fish-loving Bengalis, this is a cherished delicacy. The fish head is fried, broken into pieces and added to roasted moong dal, its copious brain matter (like the marrow from beef bones) giving a baroque note to the redolence of turmeric, ginger, cumin, cinnamon, cardamom and green chillies.

But amid the happy exuberance, I feel a deep sadness as I think of my own family. My mother was the eldest daughter among many siblings, and her wedding was a lavish affair. The legendary chef my grandfather hired for the occasion transformed the entire roof of the ancestral house into an enormous kitchen for three days. It was said that he prepared an akhni water – a stock-like decoction of the various spices used in making polau – so fragrant that the entire street was enveloped in its aroma. Every item of the spectacular meal he served was described in excruciating detail whenever any wedding was discussed in our family. It sounded like a golden affair, burnished with each retelling.

By the time I was a teenager, though, these narratives evoked only a bitter irony. The golden couple of the wedding was unrecognizable in the two adults who were my parents. A terrible sense of grievance and letdown seemed to consume them much of the time, and the most unlikely event, topic, visit or comment could precipitate a marathon session of loud arguments and bitter reproaches, scorching words that walls and doors could not keep out. And then there were the silences – long, throbbing interludes of absolutely no conversation that lasted for hours, even days.

Joy, however, was not totally absent in our family. My conflicted parents shared one enthusiasm – food. She was a fabulous cook, a true artist, and he had a rare and subtle palate. He also enjoyed shopping for the season's best produce, fish and meats. Through my school and college years, I took for granted the delectable offerings on our table – slow-cooked potatoes with tamarind and asafoetida, carp in yoghurt sauce, shrimp with ground coconut and mustard, and so many others.

Despite their constant discord, my parents were also extremely hospitable, and friends and family were frequently invited to our home for meals. Among the many classic dishes for which my mother was justly famed was muror dal. Each time she made it, she waited intently for my father's reaction. Even if they were not speaking to each other, the appreciative sniff that greeted the serving of the dal on his plate and the zestful way he sucked the juices from the head were the accolades she really looked for.

Not having the maturity to sense the complex emotions that underlay my parents' endless conflict, I blamed the Indian system of arranged marriage that allowed families to match incompatible duos for life, since Hindus do not believe in divorce. Never, I resolved, would I be trapped like that. The only way to avoid it was to escape – and I did, as far away as the United States. I also exercised choice in my marriage.

But I could not escape destiny. In the late 1980s, I found myself, the first divorcée in my orthodox Hindu family, back in Calcutta, living with my parents in their rambling three-storey house. Once again, the erupting arguments and conflicts made me ponder the nature of the marital bond that held them together. But with older eyes, I could see the deep attachment below the surface. How had it developed when they seemed to have disappointed each other right from the beginning?

One evening, when I came home from work and found them bickering viciously over a particularly insignificant matter, I lost my usual restraint. 'Why didn't you get a divorce years ago?' I burst out. 'At least I would have had some peace!'

Immediately, I was overcome with shame and regret. Didn't I know how impossible it was for people of their generation to even think about divorce? Hadn't I shamed them enough with mine? Guiltily, I fled upstairs. But my mother followed me. With surprising calmness, this habitually no-nonsense, even prosaic, woman sat down and explained her conception of marriage.

'You didn't care for our rituals,' she smiled sadly. 'You married outside our religion; you had a civil marriage in America. But you've seen many Hindu weddings. You know the ceremony requires the couple to feed the fire, and then feed each other. Food is life, and by eating together, the pair bonds for life. We did that. How can you talk to us about getting a divorce?'

She spoke of ceremony and bonds. But looking at her face, and listening to her voice, I heard only the word love. I thought back to the long years of conflict, but also to the deep, shared passion for the art of cooking, eating and offering hospitality. That daily tableau of the table, I now saw, was neither duty nor obligation – it was love, but a tormented version that found no expression except through food.

Soon after, I went away again – back to America. After my father's death, I decided to bring my mother over to join me, and for ten years I watched as time and distance failed to wipe out her regrets and sorrows. In the absence of the one person with whom she had argued and fought and eaten, she totally lost the pleasure she once took in cooking. Even her enjoyment of food seemed sadly diminished.

The wedding I am attending in Calcutta – an arranged marriage – is in the evening. By now, I am in a pensive mood. The tatto has been put away, the fish consumed by the family. In the large rented hall, a canopied enclosure has been decorated with red cloth and tuberose garlands. In front of the chief actors, seated on a carpet, is an array of items necessary for the complex Hindu ceremony. I see the bowl of snowy white popped rice, the bunch of ripe bananas, the conch-shaped sweets on a terracotta plate – and my mother's words ring vividly in my ears: 'Marriage is a lifelong undertaking to eat together.'

First the bride's father has to give her away. The priest guides him through the Sanskrit mantras, while he holds his daughter's hand and places it on top of the groom's. It is a solemn undertaking, since the 'gift' is not simply a daughter but also a woman now endowed with her share of the family property. The pinched look on the father's face demonstrates the effects of a day-long fast. Earlier, I had seen him at home, closeted with the household gods and one of the priests, making sacred offerings to both gods and ancestors, asking them to bless his daughter and son-in-law.

In my mother's time, the bride, too, had to fast all day. But this twenty-first-century bride had been allowed a little snack in the middle of the day. Wrapped in a gold-embroidered red silk sari, decked out in intricate gold jewellery, her forehead decorated with patterns of sandalwood paste, she seems an icon of happy expectation. Had my mother, too, looked like that on her wedding day?

Once the bride has been given away, the father leaves the scene – a symbolic gesture of renunciation. Now it is the couple's turn to wind their way through further intricate rituals, guided by two priests. Several times they make offerings to the gods: flowers, leaves, unmilled rice, a type of grass called durba. But the crucial – and most spectacular – part of the ceremony comes later. The pair rise and stand, she in front. His arms come around her and he places his palms underneath hers so that they can jointly hold a plate laden with foods. One of the priests quickly builds a fire in a large copper vessel and the couple pour offerings into it. The popped rice is the first. As it falls, the flames rise up with a whooshing sound, as if Agni, the god of fire, is welcoming the tribute. Item by item, all the food is submitted to the flames. Finally, the two walk around the fire seven times, the shoulder end of her sari knotted to his shawl, reciting the Sanskrit couplets that express the undertaking of a lifelong bond. But this first day's ceremony (weddings are not complete until the end of the third day) is not over yet. Tradition requires them to feed each other sweets from the same plate. As they do so, I am struck by the tenderness with which he brushes the crumbs from her mouth.

Throughout the long ceremony, guests have come and gone, sampling the wedding feast in another room. When most people have left, the bridal pair sit down to dinner at a large table with a group of friends. I wish them happiness and say goodbye to the family. From the landing, I look back one last time. Amid the laughter and chatter of the friends, the groom is placing a spoonful of polau on the bride's plate. She, still feeling shy, looks down, but the flush of pleasure on her cheeks and the upward curve of her mouth are unmistakable.

Suddenly, I imagine my parents in place of this couple. In my vision, their faces are fresh, expectant and youthful, instead of marked with half a century's wear and tear. I see my father, his handsome face topped by the conical groom's hat, serving portions of food onto his new bride's plate. I watch my habitually stern mother transformed into a bashful bride who smiles with happiness under the cover of her veil.

I walk away, but as I go I wish for the young couple that today's shared communion will be allowed to blossom, that the shining bride will have the uninhibited freedom to say she loves her husband and children every time she serves a meal, and that the groom will find a way to reciprocate. I wish for them a home where two people live an ordinary life, its disappointments made bearable by the leavening of laughter and the communion of food. It does not seem too much to ask.

## Muror Dal

### Ingredients

- a whole head of carp (weighing about 1 kilogram) – ask the fishmonger to clean it thoroughly, removing the gills, and cut it into four pieces, the two sides and the central back portion divided into two. It is important that the fish head be very fresh.
- approximately 500 grams yellow moong dal
- 3 medium onions ground to a paste
- 2 teaspoons freshly ground ginger
- 1½ teaspoons turmeric powder
- 3 bay leaves
- 3 whole cardamom pods
- 3 whole cloves
- 3 one-inch pieces of cinnamon sticks
- 4 whole green chillies, slit down the middle
- 5 tablespoons mustard oil
- salt to taste

## Process

Roast the moong dal in a wok or pan over medium heat, stirring continuously until the grains turn light brown in colour and a pleasant aroma fills the kitchen. Remove from fire and keep aside. Take the pieces of fish head, wash thoroughly, and dust them with half a teaspoon of salt and the turmeric powder. Toss in a bowl to coat the pieces properly.

Heat 1½ tablespoons of oil in a wok and sauté the fish head pieces for 4 to 5 minutes over medium-high heat. There will be a lot of spatter, so use a net lid to control it. Remove from heat and lift out the pieces.

Heat a clean cooking pot, pour in the rest of the oil and throw in the bay leaves, cardamom, cloves and cinnamon. After one minute, when the spices give out their fragrance, add the grated onions and ginger and sauté until the mixture turns reddish brown. Add the roasted moong dal and pour in 4 cups of hot water. Add salt. Keep covered until the mixture comes to a boil.

Add the pieces of fish head and cook, covered, over medium heat until the dal is soft and mushy. The fish heads will also soften and you can break them into smaller pieces with your spatula. Check for salt, adding if needed, throw in the green chillies, and simmer for

2 to 3 minutes to allow the flavours to blend and the chillies to impart some heat to the dal.

Remove and serve with plain rice.

N.B. The water can be adjusted according to your preference for the consistency of the dal. Some people like a touch of tart in this dal. You can add a bit of tamarind paste (mixed with water) or lime juice and blend it in before taking the dal off the stove.

# ENDINGS

# Transformed by Fire

IN THE DESERTED CAMBRIDGE CEMETERY, THE WIND cut into me like a scalpel – precise and ruthless – detaching me from my lifelong consciousness of being a cherished child. I trudged uphill until I reached my destination – the crematory beside the chapel. Inside, my mother's body, in a simple covered casket, lay on a table in front of the incinerator.

Cremation was the natural end for her, a devout Hindu. But in her native Calcutta, she would have been wearing a new sari, her face adorned with fragrant sandalwood paste, her body covered with flowers and wreaths. En route to the crematorium, she would be accompanied by family, friends and former students. Until the moment when she was placed on the fire, she would be visible. In Calcutta, it is hard to be alone, even in death. In Cambridge, she only had me, her sole child, gazing at a nondescript container with the word 'Head' printed at one end and her name at the other in large capital letters. Instead of a new sari, she was probably dressed in the blue-and-white robe she wore the last time I saw her in the hospital.

I reflected on her adult life, starting from her wedding during the turbulent times of Gandhi's Quit India movement, her conflicted relationship with her husband, her reluctant embrace of a full-time career as a high-school English teacher when all she wanted was to be a stay-at-home mother, the centring of her hopes and desires on the only late-arriving child she had and, through the course of years, her having to deal with the unconventional actions of that child. I thought of the disappointments some of my decisions had brought her and was filled with renewed admiration for the way she had overcome her own prejudices and anxieties and come to appreciate the relevance of my choices for my own life. When I returned to Calcutta nineteen years after I had first left as a young student, she had let herself hope that I would settle there permanently. Instead, after a few years, she had to accept her daughter's second marriage – this, too, somewhat unconventional, though not as much as the first one. My decision to leave for America again, with my husband Jai, blew away her hopes of having me near her for the rest of her life. Yet, she put them away with grace and gave me her blessings. Maybe that is why fate gave her the one thing she wished for. My father's death soon after my marriage precipitated circumstances that led me to bring her over to live with us. At the age of seventy-four, she started a new chapter of life as an immigrant. Now, twenty years later, she and I were together in the antechamber where the remembered life, the irrevocable death and the impending corporal dissolution would create the finality of her story.

The crematory attendant said I could spend some time with her – but not too long – before he pushed the casket inside and turned on the switch. I tried to imagine the ferocity of the blaze the switch would generate. In traditional Hindu funerals the body is placed on a wood pyre which is doused with clarified butter that serves as an offering to the gods and also intensifies the flames. In modern Indian crematoriums, electric burners provide a welcome alternative for many. But I had never seen a cremation, wood-fired or electric. Nor did I wish to see it now. Instead, all I could think of doing was to place my hand on the casket where I thought her heart might be and read aloud a passage from the Bhagavad Gita before saying goodbye for the last time.

The cremation would take several hours. Unable to find a suitable place to sit at the crematory, I decided to go home and continue reading from the text until the process was complete.

The bitter February chill seeped in through layers of warm clothes as I sat on my living room couch and read. I tried to focus on the text, but my eyes kept seeing the fire that was consuming my mother. The Sanskrit verses did offer temporary solace. Nothing, they said, can hurt the soul, neither the sharpest of weapons nor the hottest of flames. Maybe. But it was the reality of the body that haunted me, the body that had brought me forth, the body I had held and touched so often through long years filled with love, laughter, anger, expectation, disappointment and sorrow – that body was now undergoing a fiery transformation into something unrecognizable. Even a river of tears could not quench that fire and bring her back.

I continued reading. But as I reached a later chapter, I felt the irretrievability of my loss even more deeply. The magnificent verses described how Krishna the deity permitted Arjuna the warrior to see the infinite, malleable and manifold nature of divinity. In that vision, a thousand flames burned bright and consumed past, present and future as they rushed towards their fate like rivers to the sea. It was a vision of inhuman beauty that I found unbearable. I had to turn away from the text.

As a child, I had always been fearful of fire until I

was old enough to spend time in my mother's Calcutta kitchen. On this icy night of bereavement, I found myself there again, without knowing how. The flickering blue flames of the gas stove were a welcome vision that evoked her culinary wizardry. I saw her hands, those magician's hands, making one of my favourite items, the Bengali fried bread called luchi. No one made luchis like my mother. She rolled out little balls of dough into thin discs, while the oil heated in the karai. She picked up the first disc and lowered it into the hot oil with a supremely elegant motion. I watched as the disc puffed up with air and floated in the dark interior of the karai like a full moon sailing in the night sky. She transferred the luchi to a plate and handed it to me. I punctured the thin top layer with a finger and a fragrant steam entered my nose and mouth as I inhaled deeply. I ate the luchi, bit by delicious bit, while she rolled out more discs from the dough. When she looked to see if I was ready for another, the only flame I saw was that of the love in her eyes.

# Empty Table

SHORTLY AFTER MY HUSBAND, JAI, DIED OF A SUDDEN, violent early morning heart attack on Christmas Day, I sat in the hospital with two friends, overcome by a sense of unreality. This was not how it was supposed to be. He was active, full of life, and apparently healthy. As the older partner, I had always assumed I would die first and he, as a physician, would be there for me, helping me exit via a 'good' death. How could this have happened, screamed the irrational part of my mind. Why should I be confronted by the irony of a cardiologist succumbing to cardiac failure without being able to benefit from all the modern medical revival techniques he had practised so often on others? At the same time, a quieter, dispirited voice reminded me that there is no predictability about individual endings.

And then I heard the word. One of my oldest friends was on the phone, cancelling plans with someone so he could be here for me. I heard him mid-sentence: '… yes, it is quite shocking … he was young and healthy … and, as I am sure you understand, I can't be at your place today. Right now, I am in the hospital with his widow.'

Widow. That was how I was being referred to by someone who had known me for decades – as a graduate student, a working woman, a married woman, a divorced woman, a woman married for the second time, a journalist, an editor, a writer, a cook. All those other identities, built up over the years, were brushed aside by the brutal power of a word loaded with centuries of cultural negativity. I remembered the widowhoods I had witnessed intimately in my life – those of my grandmother and my mother. In 1995 I had written a piece about widowhood for *Granta*, 'What Bengali Widows Cannot Eat'. In spite of some reluctance to expose the personal suffering of the women I deeply loved, I had been compelled, as a food writer, to reveal to readers the particular iniquity that has been visited on the Hindu widows of Bengal. For centuries, these unfortunate women, particularly those belonging to the upper castes, were penalized for something over which they had no control – the death of their husbands – and now having to submit to a lifetime of deprivation. Many of the things that formed part of their diet, nutritious items like fish, meat, eggs, lentils and other items, became forbidden food. Draped with the mantle of inauspiciousness, dressed in unrelieved white, they were irrationally blamed for the cruel fate of their own widowhood, and often subjected to domestic drudgery. Widows in Bengal were condemned to what was less than a half-life for their remaining years.

Although social and cultural norms have changed significantly in recent times and Bengali widows are no longer penalized with strict dietary restrictions, the aura of negativity that surrounds the image of the widow has not totally disappeared. My friend's words transformed me from a person into a widow, raising the spectres of the past while bringing home one of the many ways my present and my future had been transformed. Sure, my life in America was not subject to the rules of tradition, custom or religion, but there was no escaping the awareness that from now on I would be confronting the stark solitude of an empty table. This was permanently inescapable.

Solitude and I are not strangers, nor have we always been adversarial. Growing up as the only child of a working mother, I was used to being on my own. As an adult, unmarried or divorced, I adjusted to the single state with more ease than many of my friends. And during my married years, when the particular demands of Jai's profession meant that we spent part of the week in two different places, I had succeeded in creating a routine adequately filled with work and social activities for the days I spent by myself. The only thing that posed a problem during those days was eating alone. I got around it by never sitting at the table for meals. Instead, I occupied the couch in front of the television or the chair in front of the computer. The very modern pleasures of watching movies and TV programmes on streaming services were particularly welcome as they made me less conscious of being a solitary diner.

Meanwhile, the table, though unoccupied by plates and edibles, signalled the pleasurable prospect of meals to be shared with Jai when he returned home, and with friends whenever they joined us for dinner. It was a bare surface that I knew would be embellished with the stuff of life at regular intervals.

Meals with Jai, even the simplest weeknight ones, were always accompanied by protracted conversation. They often reminded me of the very first time the two of us had dinner together in a restaurant in Calcutta, when we suddenly discovered that we were the last remaining customers and the staff were politely waiting for us to leave at the end of almost three hours. We had consumed the food and, in the process, had been almost consumed by our words. And so it continued to be over the years we spent together. An infinite range of topics made their way to our table, from people, to politics, to my work as a food historian and his as a physician. Even on our worst days, I cannot recall having a meal with Jai in glowering silence.

Suddenly, all the words were gone. All I was left with was an irrevocable silence.

Since that fatal Christmas morning, I have tried to find ways to combat the silence and transform the emptiness of my table, at least in my mind, into one of the many images of meals past. Momentary comfort touches me, but not strong enough to recreate a new way of sitting down to a meal full of pleasure. I go through the motions, since life requires that. I chop vegetables, I heat the pan, I throw in spices, I cook. I remind myself that Jai was never an advocate of mourning and isolation. He had shown little patience with those who gave in to excessive, paralyzing sadness. The claims of life, he said, took precedence over those of death. Had he been around, he would urge me to think of the next book I would write, or to research a little-known corner of the world with an as yet unrevealed food culture.

He would remind me of a Bengali story he loved, which I had read aloud to him one winter evening. A young boy, home with his aunt while his parents are out for dinner, accidentally finds a pair of tongs with the magical power to summon a demon. When the demon appears and asks what they want, the boy asks for a bag of hot, roasted chickpeas, while his aunt asks for lots of gold jewellery which can be part of her wedding dowry. The demon obliges. As they munch on the chickpeas, the aunt suddenly wonders if this is a dream, if she will wake the next day to find that all the jewellery has disappeared. Her nephew wisely tells her that even if that happens, nothing can take away the delicious chickpeas once they have eaten them. This is a memory that lifts my mood. Nothing can take away the meals and the words I have already shared with Jai. I go to bed and fall asleep quickly.

The bedroom door opens. Barely awake, in the filtered light of early morning, I see Jai walk in and sit on the bed. I am surprised. He had been on call for the hospital the night before and was not supposed to be back so soon. It must have been an easy night, I think. 'Get up,' he says, smiling, 'I brought croissants and coffee – let's have breakfast.'

I get out of bed and walk to the dining table. There are no croissants and coffee, of course, but for the first time since Christmas I do not feel oppressed as I look at the table. He had come to me in a dream, a gift of profound kindness – from my own self or from the presence he had been for thirty years of my life – filling the void with the generosity of shared sustenance.

# Sources

A different version of 'Petal Vessel' was published in *Departures*, (Special issue, "India Now", New York, October 2008.)

A slightly different version of 'Small, Round Things' was first published in *Gastronomica* (Berkeley: University of California Press, Fall 2005).

A slightly different version of 'A Sweet Fragrance in Winter' was published in *Gastronomica* (Berkeley: University of California Press, Spring 2012).

'Tea with My Father' was originally published in *Teabox.com* on 14 February 2016.

'Dining on Faith' was originally published in *Gourmet* (New York, February 2002).

A different version of 'Green Noodles by the River' was published in *Traveller* (London, Summer 2009).

'Seeds of Dreams' was originally published in *Gourmet* (New York, August 2003).

'A Shared Plate' was originally published in *Gourmet* (New York, November 2005), and reprinted in *The Best American Travel Writing 2006* (New York: Houghton Mifflin Company, 2006).

A different version of the following recipes was published in *Bengali Cooking* (New Delhi: Aleph Book Company 2017, published by arrangement with New York: OR Books/Serif):

Mochar Ghanto
Payesh
Chirar Polau
Chitol Kopta
Kadam Bhai's Duck Bhuna
Posto Bata
Lamb with Posto

# Acknowledgements

THE PUBLICATION OF THIS BOOK WOULD NOT HAVE happened without the sustained, enthusiastic support of Teesta Guha Sarkar at Picador/Pan Macmillan India. Through the uncertainty and grimness of the pandemic, she remained unwavering in her commitment to the project. For a writer, an editor like Teesta is an extraordinary gift and I feel really fortunate to have been able to work with her. My gratitude is immense.

As always, I deeply appreciate the help and guidance of my wonderful agent, Anne Edelstein.

Lastly, I wish to thank all the friends (too many to name) who shared my joys and sorrows and faithfully stayed by my side as I dealt with the losses and desolation that have come my way over the course of my life. I owe them my survival.

# Acknowledgements